SYLVAIN PAQUETTE

THE HIDDEN FACE OF CREDIT BUREAUS

How to free yourself of debt and prosper

How to get out of debt with the Babylonian Theory

Éditions Véritas Québec

THE HIDDEN FACE OF CREDIT BUREAUS

Bibliothèque et Archives nationales du Québec and Library and Archives Canada cataloguing in publication

Paquette, Sylvain, 1970

The hidden face of credit bureaus: how to free yourself of debt and prosper with a Babylonian theory

Translation of: La face cachée des bureaux de crédit

ISBN 978-2-89571-107-0

1. Consumer credit - Québec (Province).
2. Debt - Québec (Province).
3. Finance companies - Québec (Province).
4. Finance, Personal. I. Title II. Title: Face cachée des bureaux de crédit. English.

HG3756.C3P3613 2014   332.7'4309714   C2014-941315-7

Translation by: **JoAnne Gauthier, Rev**
Proofreader: **Patrick Mercier**
Editing: **Véritas Québec**
Cover Design by: **Frédérick Beauchamp**
Graphics: **Monique Moisan • mmoisan@supernet.ca**

Publishing house: **Le Triangle d'Or * v.f**
245, de la Concorde Blvd., West
Laval (Qc) H7N 6H5
450-901-0121
www.bucc.ca

Publishing house: **Éditions Véritas Québec * v.e**
2555, ave Havre-des-Îles, Suite 118
Laval, (Qc) H7W 4R4
450-901-0121
www.editionsveritasquebec.com

Legal Deposit: Quebec National Library and Archives,
Library and Archives Canada

ISBN Printed version   978-2-89571-107-0
ISBN Numeric version   978-2-89571-108-7

This book is dedicated with all my love to my children, Marilyn and Seleyna and to all the children who will take the lead to create a better world.

PRESENTATION

"**All knowledge is a response to a question.**" This sentence is well suited to introduce the book you just opened. For philosopher Gaston Bachelard[1], dreaming of a better world and learning how to create this world through scientific knowledge is changing mankind. In the mad rush for prosperity, economic power is concentrated in the hands of the elite while the needy mass is crumbling under the weight of debt. What we ignore is, which questions to ask to change the balance of power between social unequivalence. I have thus been interested for years, whilst trying to solve my own problems, in how the banking system operates. More than ten years passed before I would be able to share the results of my findings and this, I confess, to be somewhat partial.

In the **first part** of this essay, I describe my first discovery. Because understanding the financial system was the trigger for all my other survival strategies, I dedicated my first fifty pages to this topic.

As my intention is to help people economically struggling to stay afloat in a world of financial sharks, the **second part** explains how to successfully consolidate one's vision of money and get organized in order to live without Damocles' sword, that represents the debt constantly hanging over our heads.

Finally, in the **third part**, I will also give you tips and tricks to renew prosperity and learn to manage abundance in accordance with these values which are my own. This book can be read in its entirety in order to obtain a more comprehensive view of the economic reality that surrounds us. Each part may also be useful to readers who seek more immediate answers to their questions.

In my own words, I would say that the publication of this

---

1 Bachelard, Gaston (1884-1962), was a French philosopher and psychoanalyst who loved to reconcile sciences and poetry. He notably initiated the theory of thought a critical tool in the quest for knowledge. *Le Nouvel Esprit scientifique*. Éditions Alcan 1934.
Source: http://fr.wikipedia.org/wiki/Gaston_Bachelard

book has allowed me to demonstrate to thousands of people that "the truth sets us free." Faced with financial difficulties, guilt and despair await those who are stuck in a system created for policymakers. What we do not know, is that the banking system has chosen us to be seated in the Victims chair and has created the conditions to ensure that we remain imprisoned in that position for as long as possible. Are you determined to end this hell of debt? Then without further delay let's get into the heart of the matter.

TABLE OF CONTENTS

INTRODUCTION

I was born in the middle of a Cultural Revolution, when society moved from subsistence farming to mass production, with the introduction of consumption as the generator of success. Obviously, there were established social classes, and I was part of the middle class, with hard working parents with strong Judeo-Christian values of mutual aide and moderation, yet unable to make ends meet. Obtaining wealth was not always well perceived, nor was drowning in debt and going bankrupt. Questions rarely arose in regards to the relationship between power and capital. My parents believed that education could make a difference and so, they encouraged me to do better by learning what they were so lacking. Knowledge is power...

After kicking and screaming my way through the "school of life" rather than educational institutions, I gradually got stuck in the spiral of odd jobs. The desire to have that false freedom that credit and the idea of " "luck" created, found me in limbo the next day because I didn't believe at the time that it committed me to failure. This inspired some serious introspection as to why I was in such deep water and how I could find a way out. Fortunately, curiosity got the best of me. I found myself passionately interested in the banking system as I climbed up the gears of this vast and powerful machine that continuously left me to be the one in a state of owing rather than the one enriching himself. My first questions will seem crazy to those who have studied in administration ... But for most people, these are the answers to the questions that can shed light on the reasons for debt enslavement, as I myself have endured for a long time.

- Who creates the money?
- On what value is it based?
- Where do our taxes and income tax funds go?
- What is bank secrecy?
- What is the bank split?
- What is securitization?
- What is a credit bureau?

- Who owns the Bank of Canada or the Federal Reserve?
- Where does the loan money come from?

My goal is to highlight certain information to help restore balance between the consumer and the financial system controlled by the banks. Don't get me wrong, I'm not trying to dump the weight of my own mistakes on the bank system: throwing the first stone will not change the debt spiral in any way. But I think that we have to face the ways and customs of this environment to understand the pitfalls and avoid them as much as possible. For our ignorance, our individualism, our desire to own property that exceeds our means creates more powerful banking institutions, able to crush us when we make the wrong decisions. Finding yourself in financial difficulties is a painful phase, where a deep questioning begins, an open door to sometimes an unsavoury way out where abusers will sink you even deeper rather than reach out to you with a helping hand.

The hidden face of the credit bureaus will tell you how the system works as you discover the backstage of this theater known as our current banking system. You will find in this book, information on the credit system, its history, its goals and how it operates. My goal is to reach out to you with a helping hand, illuminating the way and equipping you with the proper tools as you make those important choices and decisions. When I realized that knowledge gave me back the power to get out, and that this power would yield a more stable life, the realization of my projects in a good way and the feeling of security, I was suddenly on the right path. I now encourage you to follow the path I took, knowing that it is up to each to find their own answers.

So here's where it all began ... There was a point in my life when I was in a more rebellious mode, where I saw conspiracies everywhere and I cursed banks, our politicians and government. Then one day I met a wonderful lady who offered me her business coaching services. This lady brought me to meet other groups of people involved in the personal growth and development industry and that is where I learned and decided to live my life according to values based on beauty, goodness and truth. So I built a new scale of values and I chose to devote my life to good causes.

One day, during an exchange with my life coach, I expressed my sense of injustice in regards to our banking system, our politicians, our governments that fill their pockets, the lobbyists, the influential trafficking, collusion, corruption and the litany that goes on daily when everything goes wrong for us. She asked me one fundamental question that changed the direction of my life thereafter, "Do you vote Sylvain?" That set me off: "No, because it's the same old, same old, nothing changes"... I said scornfully. Without letting me finish my sentence, striking a firm fist on the table, she replied: "Then shut up!" in a determined tone. I was speechless, then she went on:" You complain against banks, against the system and against the government and you don't even vote? What are you personally doing to improve society? What are you leaving behind for your children to inherit? Instead of playing the Victim, become an advocate for change... Be the one that creates change, otherwise shut up.

A famous sentence from Gandhi came to me in that moment: "Let us be the change we want to see in the world." This is the trigger event that changed my life and led me to write this book.

The truth will set you free... When it comes to earning a good living and establishing financial security, learning the rules of the game makes all the difference. A prime example is the creation of the Desjardins Group. At the end of the race for wealth, there is only one winner and many losers, just like in the game of Monopoly. Our current lifestyle based on consumerism, individualism and the adulation of "money" like a God, has pushed values such as the advancement of humanity into second place. Money is less and less of service to collective development. The future, however, rests on altruism and sharing resources with communities. There is enough wealth on earth for all to eat and live decently. A reporter recently published, that if the loans to U.S. banks by Congress had been distributed among all human beings, each would have received over a million dollars! We're a long way from the practice of "equitable sharing". Thus by leaving our fate in the hands of bankers, as is the present **case**, we will end up crushed under the weight of our debt, their royalties. It is our duty to change things from individualistic to collective thinking, so as to serve others and work for the benefit of the community, for the wellbeing of all. Every day we meet people who reflect the individualistic line of thought of "every man for himself." My perspective is to end the "me, myself, and I" way of thinking and to defend and support the "we, us and others." The principle of "pay it forward" is a good example of the beneficial emotions that can occur in humans.

The cash pump sucks us in... Who benefits from our consumer frenzy? Filling the government coffers with the various taxes collected on goods and services sold, indeed fattening financiers. In order for the cash pump to efficiently flow, be profitable and in constant production mode, you must create one or more NEEDS. Besides advertising and marketing, the desire to consume must be motivated by a recurring pattern at the core of the system. A state of psychological distress, a false desire to pamper yourself will compel you to acquire consumer goods to alleviate your discomfort, "because you deserve it as much as others", say advertisers. Buying under emotional stress of the moment and not taking the time to contemplate your action, will lead you into debt.

If you study them you will find that all corporations exploit this pattern in order to be profitable. The military system, medical, food, legal, psychiatric, religious, banking, pharmaceutical... commonly promote the feeling of "If I buy this it will make me happy. Let's look more closely at this spiral based on acquisition. All day long you play the role of desiring what publicity is offering you without even realizing it. Take a blank sheet of paper and draw a triangle. At the top of the triangle write *Persecutor,* at the bottom left, *Rescuer,* and at the bottom right,

Victim. This triangle is also known as the Karpman Triangle[2] or better known as the drama triangle. Look around and you'll recognize people in your environment playing these roles. A common example is when you are at a family dinner. Notice the **Victim** is <u>the person who always complains</u>.e.g. bad things only happen to him, she always sees the negative side of things, she was born into a life of poverty, his life is a dark series of events that is repeated endlessly, she draws to herself the perpetual drama situations and so on it goes.

The Rescuer is easy to recognize, he's the happy-go-lucky person that wears his heart on his sleeve, who wants to help everyone and will even go to the point of meddling into the affairs of others. He or she always ends up duped.

The Persecutor is the one who is afraid of being duped and protects himself with a shell. He projects onto others his anger as well as everything he does not like about himself, and accuses everyone because he feels Victimized.

Inevitably, whatever role you play, you always end up as a Victim. Generally, one of three functions is more dominant than the other in a person, and these roles become your comfort zone. However, even if a role is more dominant in an individual, we are called to play all three roles and several times a day without even realizing it.

---

2   The drama Triangle, also known as Karpman Triangle, is a transactional analysis figure proposed in 1968 by Stephen Karpman highlighting a typical relationship scenario between Victim, Persecutor and Rescuer (since these roles are symbolic, the same person can change roles). Source: http://fr.wikipedia.org/wiki/Triangle_dramatique

Here is an illustration of the Karpman triangle and the definition of the three roles.

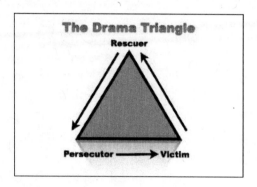

The "Drama Triangle" game. A game is a series of exchanges where the protagonists are unknowingly set up in predetermined roles. The *Persecutor* in his exaggerated form attracts to himself the *Rescuer* and the *Victim*. He projects his anger and pain on his helpless Victim, whom he criticizes and demolishes. The Persecutor uses the Victim as a sponge to absorb the surplus of anger and frustration in addition to his many other unconscious emotions. He feels obliged to be very harsh and nasty. He abuses his power and exposes the flaws of his Victim. This is the only unconscious behaviour he possesses to empower himself, because he often has very little self-esteem. The character of the Persecutor is defined by behaviour: moralistic, overbearing, brute, violent, castrating, demeaning. The following are some typical Persecutor phrases:

> *Mine is better than yours*
> *Now I want my revenge*
> *You wouldn't be in this mess if you had listened to me*
> *I don't want to hurt you, but I'll be honest with you*
> *You are like this and like that*
> *You just don't understand*
> *Imbecile!*

In regards to finances, the person whose dominant role is the Persecutor has been a Victim of either financial loss or has lived in fear of lack. He or she blames others for their misfortune and continues to make decisions based on emotions and often makes bad investments. When this person talks about his money, you feel his anger. He will easily judge others and does not like to be questioned.

The Rescuer in his exaggerated form draws to himself both the Victim and the Persecutor. His goal is to be liked by helping others without being asked, sometimes to the extent of not even asking for consent. He will take on all the work for them, rendering them dependent and submissive. He seeks to be accepted at any cost and not to displease. He is peaceful, friendly and helpful. He avoids confrontation. He is always ready to sacrifice himself to please others. He has the feeling of never doing enough. He lives only for the recognition of others, which never comes, so sooner or later, the Rescuer inevitably becomes the Victim. This is when he complains of someone he helped and didn't acknowledge his efforts. He seeks compassion and pity and at this point he finds a new Rescuer or Persecutor. The following are some typical Rescuer phrases:

> *I'll take care of everything*
> *Tell me what's wrong, I can help you*
> *If I were you, I would ...*
> *You can count on me, I'll get you out of this*

The Rescuer in regards to his finances is usually poorly organized or completely broke and has very little financial savvy. He seeks approval and wants to be loved, so he tries to help his family and loved ones to recover from their own situations. He lends or gives money without thinking about his own needs. He has a strong desire for recognition. The Rescuer can spot a good deal and will blindly plunge into it and will usually associate with other Victims to help them with their business, which eventually brings him right back to being the Persecutor.

The Victim, in his exaggerated form, tends to overplay his troubles by presenting them as greater than they really are, which in turn draws to him a Rescuer and a Persecutor. This allows him to remain in his familiar comfort zone. Although he is not at ease or content to be in this situation, he remains in denial ignoring his own behaviour and continues to play the Victim role. When faced with suffering and hurtful situations, the Victim is easily identified by his attitude and constant complaining about his circumstances. He uses this method to draw the attention of the Persecutor and the Rescuer. Once he's identified his Rescuer he then receives the attention he needed to relieve his discomfort. The following are some typical Victim phrases:

> *I'm swamped with work*
> *I am alone in the world*
> *What's happening to me is terrible*
> *It's his/her fault*
> *I can't take this anymore*
> *I'll never get out of this*
> *Things like this only happen to me*

The Victim goes from one financial situation to another. As soon as he starts to climb out, he falls right back into the hole again.

To find true happiness and both financial and emotional balance, we must learn to get out of this overconsumption and debt pattern that keeps us in psycho-emotional distress. So what's the secret? It's simple and takes a little discipline, but everyone can get there in as little as a few weeks time.

The following are some important tips and advice to heighten your awareness and help develop critical thinking with respect to the emotional triangle and get you out of this destructive pattern.

1. First we must be aware of the existence of this pattern;
2. Observe behaviour in others and try to identify what role each person plays. Do this for two to three weeks;
3. During every break in the day, observe your behaviour and make a self-assessment to find out what role you

held and what role your peers held. Use this method during the fourth and fifth week.

4. Progressively change your attitude by affirming your own beliefs and refuse to stay in a role that doesn't suit you.

Remember that when you fall back into the triangle and you assume one of the roles, the resulting emotions arouse fear, doubt and confusion. This takes you straight back into emotional instability. You'll discover that by mastering the pattern, you become much more grounded and able to make decisions based on logic rather than anxious or distressed emotions. You will feel clearer about everything and avoid feelings of guilt about your actions.

You will understand that the system we operate in is based on theatrics, a grand illusion, and that by allowing yourself to be exploited, you play the role of a willing character. To free yourself, you should understand the rules of the game. Indeed, you will see more clearly and you will know to distance yourself from the Victim role, which does not serve you, yet empowers those around you. Your role in society and in the financial system is that which you choose to occupy, as an actor: you can reply and change the action to your advantage. Consider a fairly common example. A collection agency contacts you. When the agent calls, he puts his Persecutor mask on to put you in an "emotional loser" state of mind. Why does he behave in this way? He will destabilize you or intimidate you to get you to lose your ability to judge and discern. In this state of fear, doubt and confusion, you promise to pay! After this step, he becomes the Rescuer because it is thanks to him that you will save your credit. Now guess what role you fall into? That's right, you've got it. It's the Victim role! But from the point of view of the creditor, the Persecutor was you, because you didn't pay your bank notes and the collector is the Rescuer and represents the creditor. You see for each of the characters, the role is at the opposite of one another.

Learning and understanding. In order to achieve these two things you must have the ability to take a step back and look at your current situation. Yes, we need a dose of courage to face reality, but it also involves taking thoughtful action that leads us to change the things that do not suit us. By silencing your emotions you can have a better perspective of the role the system has assigned you. You have the power to change that role and opt out of the financial failure test.

PART I

UNDERSTANDING
THE FINANCIAL SYSTEM

CHAPTER 1
THE GLOBAL MONOPOLY GAME

This chapter will certainly be one that will challenge your vision of our current financial and legal system. My explanations may not suit everyone, I do not expect you to blindly believe everything I write, but I intend to open your eyes to a certain reality so you may draw your own conclusions. One day a great wise man said: "If someone seeks the truth, follow him. If someone has found the truth, flee him."

Remember when you last played the game of Monopoly, you found that there are winners and losers, is this not true? However, you quickly noticed that the bank never loses. In addition, to play, you must first borrow from the bank. You cannot play without renting (cost being interest) your money from the bank.

How many of you actually read the rules before you played? If you're like me, a mere novice, you joined the party and your comrades explained the rules as you played the game. Some of your friends may have even cheated by diverting the rules of the game to their advantage or simply invented new ones: "On this square you have to pay, don't ask questions, everyone has to pay, those are the rules." And the game continues. Then you soon realize that your friends are playing in their best interest and not yours. Until the day you decide to get the rules sheet out and say: "Those rules aren't written anywhere ? You tricked me and lied, you turned it to your advantage !" Your friends will say: "The rules were there, you just didn't read them. It was up to you to read them. It's your responsibility to be informed if you don't want to get taken advantage of."

Unfortunately, they are right. Ignorance is expensive. Have you read the rules of the Canadian banking system ? The Constitution of Canada ? The Criminal Code ? The Civil Code ? The Bank Act ? If not, you may wish to do so. Could it be that our policymakers lead us on without giving us the time of day, so our vigilance remains asleep, allowing our power to pass into the hands of the "authorities" ? Take a dictionary and look up the definition of the word "code". While a code is a set of laws and regulations according to the dictionary, it is also a kind of secret language or encrypted (coded) language used between two or more parties of initiates. How is it that some basic principles of law which are, in my opinion, of paramount importance, are not generally taught in our school system ? Are there people, companies, organizations and institutions that benefit from our ignorance to feed their personal and group interests ? Speaking from my own personal experience and expertise, I would have to say YES.

When you're a pawn in the game of Monopoly, it's difficult to see beyond the next square in front of you. When you are fully aware of the game and your hand is an extension of your consciousness (the hand holding the pawn), you have an overview of the rest of the game. My motivation is to awaken your consciousness so that you become the hand that holds the pawn and not the pawn on the game board.

Before delving into this section, put the book down and go

get your driver's license. Come on, do it and you will understand.

Look carefully and see how your name is registered. Your name is written in capital letters followed by your first name, is not it? Why is your name written in capital letters?

However, if you look at the rest of your license, the sentences have capital letters at the beginning and are followed by lowercase letters as in the text for this book. Are there any differences between, SOSTUCK GERARD and Gerard SOSTUCK? If you look on your credit cards, your tax returns, your bank notes, you will always find your name in capital letters. Why?

Yet, since grade school, you were taught to write your name in the right way, the first letter in uppercase and the rest in lowercase letters. Then, at age 16, all your documents are labelled with your name in capital letters. When a name is written in uppercase only, it means a corporation.

To play in the Canadian Monopoly system, you have to play as a corporation. The human being is somehow authorized as the representative of the corporation bearing his name in capital letters. Why all this merry-go-round ride? Why can we not function as human beings in this system?

It's simple, humans predate the state, they have inalienable rights (birthrights), while corporations have obligations and privileges that are granted by the State. That is why, in my opinion, the corporation is created by the state, unlike the human being which is created, so it is said, by God. The corporation carries the name of a legal entity, which is superimposed on the human being.

This corporation is a legal personality as set out in Article 1 of the first book of Quebec's Civil Code. As cited in the Constitution of Canada, "Whereas Canada is founded upon principles that recognize the supremacy of God and the rule of law," does this same right allow for the right to waive legitimacy, but not the law?

Always, in the concept of duality that binds "human" and "legal personality", you will find the former as creditor and the latter as debtor by default. The "human being" has the power to create, it is co-creator with God, the "human being" has all the rights without being recognized by a State. The "legal personality" is a lifeless entity, a mask created by the state and, by extension, acts on behalf of the "human being". Moreover, the word "person" originates from the Latin word "persona", meaning "theatrical terracotta mask" worn by actors.

So, to consciously play in the great drama of society, you must realize that you are wearing this mask, the mask of the "legal entity" that was given you at your birth. Here is a brief outline of this distribution...

GOD

NATURE

MAN & WOMAN

GOVERNMENT

CORPORATION & PERSON

The belief is that God created the world, he made nature, then he created man and woman, and they created the government to organize themselves in society and the government created corporations and individuals. An immutable law of the universe and recognized in the natural law is: a creature cannot prevail on its creator. But the temptation is great: perpetuate the exploitation of man by man. Is it possible that some governments have created corporations and individuals to override the laws of God for profit? Hence the importance of reintegrating our values within our economic, political, legal and social system.

You must have noticed that humanity cannot prevail over nature, because the latter always has the last word. The government is at the service of man, but can rule over his creations that are corporations and individuals. It is not the government that creates man, but nature.

In order for the government to have authority over you, you must recognize it as your creator and benefactor. It is by your consent that you agree to play the game with your "legal personality".

As you will see further, there is a rule of law that states, that if you exercise your consent in a social contract with the state, you give up what makes your constitutional rights. In the book Vie Privée et droits fondamentaux[3] (Privacy and human rights) by Alain-Robert Nadeau, lawyer and doctor of constitutional law, we read:

However, the use of subterfuge to obtain consent goes beyond the scope of consent given by an individual.

I will clarify this notion in Chapter 15, because there are limits to the conditions relative to the consent given by the consumer.

And further, Alain-Robert Nadeau writes:

Our courts rely on the origins, the constitutional traditions which precepts are enshrined in constitutions and in international treaties as well as the liberal doctrine under which the individual exists prior to the State and the individual's fundamental rights having their origin not from recognition by a State or an international organization, but rather are based upon attributes of the human person.[4]

You understand that to play the part of social Monopoly, you do not play as a human being, you play as a person (legal personality).

Look with a magnifying glass on a Canadian $50 bill. You will find a statement that says: "since 1948, women are persons". What were they before 1948? And who gives himself the right to define this? And how could legislators hide something

---

3   A-R. Nadeau; *Vie privée et droits fondamentaux*, publications Carswell, 2000, p. 320.
4   Ibid., p. 322.

as important as the concept of defining someone or a group of people without our knowledge ? Therefore is your credit record that of your personality or yours as a human being or even as a consumer ? And when you go bankrupt, is it you or your legal status ? Can a human being come into this world with an accountable debt to the government ?

In a way, it's a form of slavery, because you must buy your freedom by paying taxes and only one year after your death will you be freed from the state. Yet slavery was banned in the 19th century, correct ? What's more docile than a slave who does not see his chains ? He will never rebel, and the master, in this case the banker will enjoy the fruit of his labour...

Unfortunately, some individuals and groups of conspiratorial nature use this concept of legal personality VS human being for profit and deceitful purposes. The reason for this information is not that you give up your "legal personality" to begin to assert your rights as a human being and avoid your responsibilities, quite the contrary. The motivation behind this is to enable you to understand the difference in order to exonerate you from feelings of guilt with respect to some financial problems and failures.

And how exactly was that legal personality assigned to me ? Be sure to read the next chapter, we'll get into the nitty-gritty.

CHAPTER 2

THE PERSONALITY'S MASK

I n this chapter I offer you my understanding from both my experience and my research of the debit-credit system. With the help of a journalist friend, we gathered information to provide you with an overview of the topic. My research goes back to 2004 but the information is still current, without being an absolute truth you may each draw your own conclusions.

Industry Canada is a department that administers the import-export to Canada, the field of insolvency and Vital Records in all provinces except Quebec. In Quebec, it is the Director of Civil Status, which administers the birth registry. Is there a link between the two? I think so.

In general, and in a vernacular language, a person is synonym for "human being" as well as the words "man" and "woman." More specifically, in regards to the Quebec Civil Code, a person is synonymous with role, social character (doctor, dentist, father, mother, divorced, married, etc..) Or personality (the Queen in person).

Who are we? Etymologically speaking, the word "person" comes from the Latin word persona meaning "character" or theater mask. The word persona, appeared around the 12th century, was later transformed into "wearer of the mask" and "character" and today "role", the social role played by subjects under the legislature of the State. If the word "role" is important it's because a person derives its personality characteristics from its status (citizen, Quebec, married).

One can also think of the Latin phrase "in corpora" (which reminds us of the characteristic of some companies) which means "in person." Incorporate literally means "for one thing to embody another." Therefore, the legal personality whose rights may be provided for, is not the man in question, but is one of its qualities incorporated into it. The human being possesses legal personality.

The Merriam-Webster dictionary defines a person as "one that is recognized by law as the subject of rights and duties, which therefore comes under legal personality." Note that the rights will be conferred by the State to the legal personality to which the person will be liable and will have obligations.

Under Article 2 of the Civil Code of Quebec, all persons hold a heritage. The person also has the option of ester (go to court) to justice. Only entities with legal personality (or moral) have this capability. Persons exercise their civil rights under the name assigned to them in the vital records (birth registry). Under other sections of the Code, this name is an event name: this is the name that endows men with legal personality.

How to define it? The question is neither existential nor theological. It does not attempt to determine the origins of man or the reasons that led to his existence, it is rather linguistic.

Knowing what we are, or rather who we are, is to seek and understand the rights and responsibilities associated with this "personality", this type of Being.

An employee of company X, when dealing with his tasks, is subject to the laws of his boss, as well as municipal, provincial, federal ... In this hierarchy of courts there are different laws that can sometimes come into conflict, but ultimately it is the highest standing law that will apply. To better swim in the sea of laws, we must know our rights.

An old expression states that "if you do not know your rights, you do not have any," even though, in theory, the ignorance of a law does not cause prejudice to that law. In other more prosaic terms, if you do not request your entitlements, who will ask for them in your place?

How to write a person's name? All documents that I've researched up to this date, all seem to agree on this point: the name of a human being must be written with the first letter in uppercase (S) and the following in lowercase (ylvain). However, you can see that corporate names are written entirely in capital letters followed by symbols such as © copyright or ®registered. Yet, when a North American looks at his name on his credit cards, driver's license, health insurance card, phone bill or electricity bill, he can see that his personal name is written entirely in capital letters without exception, just like any corporate name.

The standard for a human being is to write only the first letter of each name in uppercase[5]. So, my name should be written this way: Sylvain Paquette, and therefore any other variant (SYLVAIN PAQUETTE PAQUETTE SYLVAIN, S. PAQUETTE, etc..) is incorrect.

Now, why do all the companies mentioned above write my name as follows: PAQUETTE SYLVAIN or another variant? A name all in uppercase letters is a business name or company (GMC, WAL-MART, FUTURE SHOP, etc..).

Article 55 of the Québec Civil Code clearly states that: "Everyone has the right to respect for his name." In addition, the following article, states that anyone who uses a name other than his own is responsible for any confusion or prejudice that may result. You understand that I do not want to be held responsible for anything not being associated with my name, S. Paquette or Sylvain G. Paquette which are not Sylvain Paquette.

Would Pierre Tremblay want to stand liable for the debts incurred by Pierre P. Tremblay or P. Tremblay, without knowing that it's not Peter, or Pete Peterson Tremblay? You see how even tiny errors can be very costly. Unfortunately, credit agencies commit such errors. They cause harm to the credit ratings

---

5   Le français au bureau, 6e édition, Les Publications du Québec.

of the person who ends up with information that doesn't concern them in their credit file.

Perhaps there are still some amongst you, who remain doubtful of the real difference for example, between SYLVAIN PAQUETTE and Sylvain Paquette. Very well then, to those, I suggest reading a judgment in a case from May 28th 2004 Quebec Courthouse (Civil Division), presided by Judge François Godbout.[6] The uppercase letters are reserved for the names of legal persons.

The birth of the legal personality. Legal personality is the central concept of the Canadian and Quebec law, even if it is in fact rarely mentioned in the literature of legal reference. Yet, as we have seen, it is the basis of the Quebec justice system, since it is able to condition, regulate and define the mechanisms of any political, economic, social and commercial unit in Quebec.

> *In Quebec, it is at birth (characterized by the "full and complete extraction of the body of the foetus from the womb of his mother") that human being or child (originally foetus) obtains legal personality, the ability of having legal rights and duties. With it, he can exercise his civil rights in Quebec, contained in the Quebec Civil Code - and it is also under this same personality that he will be subjected to 62 million Canadian laws and regulations.*

Article 1 of the Quebec Civil Code states that: "Every human being possesses juridical personality and has the full enjoyment of civil rights." If one focuses the choice of words used in this article, note that every "human being" is not a legal personality, but he "owns" or "possesses" legal personality. It is important to make the distinction.

That is why, earlier, I added the following clarification: a human being can have legal personality, but "he" is not the legal personality. This personality is, in fact, a mask the human

---

6 In this trial no 200-22-028373-041, Judge Godbout mentions in particular that "Mr. Jacques-Joseph-Pierre-Antoine: Normandin, acting as representative authorized Jacques Normandin

being wears in society.

Article 5 of the Code states: "Any person exercises his civil rights in the name that is assigned to him and stated in his birth certificate"...

In the preliminary provisions of the Quebec Civil Code, it is mentioned that the "person" is born, appears with the creation of the birth certificate. We do not exercise our civil rights as "sovereign creatures of God", but as a person (character) born of the registration of birth recorded in the civil status register. A legal person is an object that has no religion, a legal person is not baptised, it has a social insurance number (SIN) and is subject to the laws.

The majority of Canadian government agencies such as the Quebec Revenue Agency, the Canadian Revenue Agency or the Bank of Canada, for example, are artificial persons.

In addition, Article 2 of the law specifies that the Governor General of Canada[7] or any other senior official representing the Canadian government for and on behalf of the Crown, is an artificial person (corporation). The Great Seal affixed on all state documents such as proclamations and commissions ministers, senators, judges and senior officials of the federal government is its distinguishing mark, logo, trademark, constituent to all artificial persons.

In order to pursue the issue, the term corporation in the Grand terminological dictionary of the Quebec Office of the French Language (http://www.granddictionnaire.com) is considered an Anglicism and in Quebec, it has been standardized, and thus the term "artificial person"[8] must be used in its place. Artificial persons are divided into two groups (private law, public law) and should be distinguished from natural persons (human beings with legal personality under Article 1 of CCQ).

Meanwhile, the American Heritage Dictionary defines the

---

7 Le gouverneur général étant le représentant de la Couronne au pays ainsi que le possesseur du pouvoir exécutif administratif et protocolaire.
8 See articles 298 to 320 of the Québec Civil Code

corporation in these words: "A group of people combined into or acting as one body. [...] A body created for purposes of government. Also called corporate body." In other words, any political grouping of government hierarchy organized in a common commercial purpose must be regarded as an artificial person, a company.

Knowing that our Civil Code is based in part on French law and more specifically on the Napoleonic Code, I would like to quote reference from two books I found dealing with the subject. One entitled Explanation of the Napoleonic Code, dating from 1804 and the other "Principe de droits civils" dating from 1887 containing all critical analysis and jurisprudence on the subject.

In Article 288 of Explanation of the Napoleon Code we read this;

"Everyone agrees that people are called civil fictitious beings. Who has the right to create these fictions ¿ To ask the question is to answer it, so the answer is unanimous: the legislature alone can create civilians. The word "create" is an ambitious word that does not fit in weak human understanding: man does not even comprehend "creation". Here, however, the word is in its rightful place, in a certain sense. At the voicing of the legislature, a being comes out of nothingness and stands equally next to real beings created by God. This means that everything is fictional in this concept."

In the *Traité des personnes* de Pothier, Part 1, Title VII, Article 2, you can read this about civilians:

"They do not have and can not have what constitutes the essence of the human personality and freedom. Man is free in everything he does, while the alleged civilian always wears chains: he may acquire, dispose of, contract, petition only with authorization, or by completing the formalities prescribed by law."

Offer a different vision. At the moment, you're probably wondering about the relevance of the information contained in this chapter and what it has to do with your financial record.

From a theoretical point of view, the concepts presented here are interesting to know, because you could do a thesis in the nature of judicial philosophy, wouldn't you agree ? In reality, the purpose of these teachings is to give you a broader vision and the opportunity to reflect on "who we are" and how to behave in our everyday life, particularly in regards to managing our finances and credit.

Understanding the basis and workings of our economic and legal system allows us to learn to modify and to put into perspective what happens when we face a debt situation for example. In my mind, this understanding of legal concepts related to our person is useful because it gives us an expanded awareness and objectivity.

From this reasoning, can we not stay more open in response to events and difficulties that beset us ?

The objective here is certainly not to justify escaping our personal responsibilities due to our management decisions. However, this information enables us to analyze our situation from a different angle, that of reason.

Knowing that we are both a **human being** and a **legal personality**, depending on the situations of our lives, sheds some light on the whole issue. Is it not comforting to think that big corporate names have been bankrupt or have submitted a proposal ? Consequently, these entities had to choose this path in order to survive, regain control and then rebuild their empire. It's a bit the same approach to an individual who is cornered by a bad credit record. It's his person and legal entity that make a bank loan, bankruptcy or a consumer proposal.

"I lost my name !" How many times have I heard this from people who see me as an advisor for insolvency ? When you left the bankruptcy trustees office, did they take away your driver's license, passport, health insurance card ? Are you now undocumented ? Of course not !

It may be guilt releasing to know that it is only as a legal personality that we are **bankrupt** or **debtor**, from a legal standpoint.

So when there is a difficult financial situation, resulting in late payments, a proposal and even bankruptcy, this may be another way for you to view this situation. Allowing you to more calmly and rationally consider this enlightening life experience that now opens the possibility to rebuild in a different way.

Our consumer society judges people by giving them the label of bankrupt, debtor, insolvent. In welcoming people to my office, I prefer to call them human **brother or sister**. The main idea is for me to help the person regain their self-confidence, so that they can see themselves in a more positive way. Through your understanding of the concepts explained in this chapter, I propose you adopt a new attitude, which is therapeutic in itself. This exercise also serves to support people in a faster rehabilitation of their financial health. Because "**it is**" possible to leave the role of Victim.

CHAPTER 3

THE BANKER STORY

T o facilitate the understanding of our credit-debit banking system, here is a brief story that should enlighten you on how some men took control of a nation and their government. I am not the author, I was told this story by a lawyer who was very knowledgeable about the banking system.

Once upon a time there were four men living on an island somewhere in the Atlantic. They all lived happily and no one went hungry. John grew vegetables, Mark tended a herd of cattle and sheep, Claude cultivated vines and produced wine, and Frank cultivated fields of wheat and barley. All exchanged their goods and lived in peace and harmony.

One day, an old man named George arrived in a boat on the beach saying that his boat was shipwrecked and he was the only survivor.

The four islanders welcomed the frail and hungry old man with open arms. "Finally someone who can bring us aid or knowledge of another civilization!" they said. As they sat for a meal, they asked George how he'd arrived there.

George told them that in his world, he was a banker and he was carrying a treasure to another world to foster the growth, development and wealth of the latter. He managed to save the treasure from the wreck and took care of burying it on the beach to conceal it.

Excited to have a treasure on their island, the four island-ers said to George: "You could be stuck here for a long time, because this island is in the middle of nowhere and ships never land here. The chances of returning to your world are very slim. Why not stay here with us and share your treasure?"

After a long moment of reflection, the old man stood up and said:

> *Okay, I agree, tomorrow morning I'll go get the treasure on the beach! Besides, I have no other choice.*

The next morning George summoned the four islanders to show them his bounty. It was a briefcase full of freshly printed green bank notes.

> *This is your treasure? What do you want us to do with these pieces of paper? We cannot cultivate the land with these paper things! exclaimed John.*

The banker replied:

> *No, no! It's just the opposite, at this moment, your crops are not maturing at the same time, so these bank notes will be used to exchange goods amongst you more easily. With these bank notes you can spend your free time building a ship, so you can then go purchase tools and rare foods in other worlds that will help you grow your riches, and you can attract people (subtly: to procure slaves) who will work for you in the fields. – This way you can relax and enjoy life instead of working by the sweat of your brow. You will become powerful and can populate your island, or even use the land on other surrounding islands. You will be prosperous and you will never run out of food.*

The four islanders asked the banker:

> *But who says that the other worlds will accept these bank notes in exchange for food or tools?*
> *It's very simple, said the banker. When I arrived on your island, I buried a chest full of gold coins! As gold is heavy and difficult to*

transport, these bank notes can be redeemed at any time against gold that is in the chest. So you will be protected against pirates when you are on a ship, and the gold will not deteriorate because it will secretly be kept in a safe place. Also, I am known in all countries by my reputation and wealth. These banknotes can be exchanged throughout the whole world, you will see for yourself, trust me."

The four islanders saw no disadvantage for them, as the banker's intention was to help them free up their time. After a brief moment of reflection, the four men said to George: "OK, we'll trust you. How does it work?"

> *Excellent! Replied George. Here's how we'll start:*
> *There are four hundred banknotes in the case, I will give you 100 bank notes each that you can then exchange amongst yourselves. As these bank notes belong to me and they are redeemable against my gold, you have to guarantee me an income. I do not cultivate the fields, I need an income to feed me and provide me food. Because these bank notes are my property, I do not ask you to pay me, give me only a pittance as compensation for these bank notes for my lending them to you.*

The four men found it honourable to pay the old man a counterpart to his generosity and ingenuity. The banker told them he would not ask for his capital back, only a 7 % interest payable at the end of the year.

"Perfect!" said the four men. At dusk, the banker went to pay the four men their fair share, one hundred beautiful green bank notes. Everyone was happy. Early the next morning, the banker went knocking on the door of each islander to ask them something...

> *Sorry to wake you up so early, but I completely forgot to have you sign our agreement for the bank notes!*

Barely able to read, John asked the banker to explain to him what was written in the document.

The banker said:

> *It is very simple, your comrades told me that you were someone*

trustworthy, but sometimes you forget, so if it ever happened that you are ill or unable to repay me your fair share of interest, I would then either have to give you more bank notes or seize your land and sell it to your comrades to reimburse myself or I rent you your land and I become owner of its title. You understand that I have full confidence in you, I proved my good faith to you by agreeing to lend you these bank notes, I have everything to lose, sir. Then it would be appropriate that you and I equally share the risk.

Of good faith and wearing his heart on his sleeve, John agreed to sign the document without really seeing the old man's real intentions.

Then the old man went to Mark, then visited Claude and finally Frank. All had affixed their signatures to the contract.

During the year that followed, the four men had established their local economy, they lived happily and prosperous. They even managed to build a boat with tools they had bought with their bank notes on another island, which allowed them to increase their respective food production.

The old man was right, the bank notes were redeemable everywhere, the four men had full confidence in their new banking partner.

Then came time to pay interest at the banker, each repaid $ 7 for the first year, for a total of $ 28 for four people. . However, there were only 372 dollars in circulation among the four people. It had no major impact on the local economy over the next year. Then our four brave people came to the end of the second year.

They reimbursed again the $ 28 dollars to the banker for the payment of interest. There were now only 344 dollars circulating in the local economy. The bank notes were becoming rare and the price of commodities began to climb. To gain the same benefit as the first year, they had to raise the prices and make everything more expensive. This is what is called inflation. The following year, the four men had to pay the sum of $ 28, as stipulated in their agreement. There now remained only 316 dollars circulating in the economy. That's it! It was a recession, nobody bought wine from Claude because it was a luxury. Claude was now unable to repay the bank on the due date. The banker said he was very sorry, but he had no choice but to seize his land and sell it to his comrades.

The other three men wanted to help their brother Claude, but did not have the necessary banknotes to purchase the land from the banker. So the banker gives them an interest-bearing loan to help them buy the land back. To secure the loan, the banker requests an additional guarantee. As the lands of the three men are already compromised by a payment guarantee, the banker requires a guarantee of payment taken directly from the profit of their crops.

Having no other choice, the three men sign the contract for a new loan. They now rent Claude's previously owned and now compromised land to Claude. Then another year passes, $100 was borrowed, but the capital was not added to the money supply, so there is now 316 dollars circulating in the local economy, the repayment of interest has passed from 28 dollars to 35 dollars.

The cost of food rises constantly every year money is scarcer and then a heavy rain comes to pass and Frank has a bad harvest of wheat and barley and finds himself unable to pay his share to the banker, who has no other choice but to seize the land from Frank and resell it to John and Mark.

Having no means to buy the land, they must sign for a new loan from the bank. Fortunately, the banker is an honest man, he has everyone's best interest at heart.

Once the four men lost their land to the banker, the latter agrees to lend them money again at a higher interest rate, because of the risk of bad debt.

Now the rate increases to 12 % interest, but the banker, concerned about the well-being of all, continues to give more loans so that the four men can begin to import and export goods on the island and not surprisingly taking guarantees on cargo ships.

As ships often sink in high seas, the banker feels the need to create a vested interest to increase profits and secure his claim. Insurance is then introduced.

A century later on the island after the old banker man was long ago dead and buried, his son continued the work of his father and the family business became a prosperous bank. All lands, all crops, all goods, in short all the riches of the island now belonged to the bank, people still work by the sweat of their brow to cultivate the land and are poorer than ever.

Once the island became an organized society, the government then signed a loan borrowing money from the bank to build roads and infrastructures. To finance its operations, the government will implement a property tax system. Then came the war and the island will be bombed and reduced to nothing. Fortunately the bombs did not hit the bank. The latter, in addition to funding the war effort, will refinance the reconstruction of the island and will provide generous loans to the people and their governments. (Remember the rumour that Nazi Germany during the Second World War or the great German bombing of London, had been financed by a bank in London and Switzerland.)

The government now having a massive debt to the bank, does not know what to offer the bank as collateral. Land, minerals, crops, etc...

The only way out for the island government will be to sell its accounts receivable to a third party (the bank). Payable year-end income tax is now withdrawn directly at the source of each taxpayer's salary to allocate the payment of interest on the government debt. The bank therefore requires the government to create a revenue agency and give it all legal and arbitrary powers to usurp the constitutional rights. The whole affair going down with the consent of the community who is under the illusion that it is to improve public services and protect the interest of the community. In this way, the government can recover its money with impunity and give interest to the banker without making the least effort. The government, having no other choice, bows to the banker for fear of losing its funding source.

Furthermore, withholding tax is no longer sufficient, because if the government raises taxes, the island will lose all its workers who will exile themselves to other countries for better opportunities. The tax increase is likely to create a civil war (it has happened), which subsequently calls for urgent intervention from the Minister of Finance. When all resources such as land, furniture and buildings were mortgaged on the island, what is there left to mortgage? Humans? Why not! Look closely at the subtlety of what follows. Of course, this doesn't happen in the public square for all to see ... It is discreetly done behind the closed doors of governments and bankers, through social contracts that you do not even suspect exist.

Centuries later, a man walking on the beach saw a chest that seemed half buried in the sand. On the chest was engraved in gold plated letters, the word "Bank". Believing he had discovered a treasure filled with gold, the man began to dig to unearth the trunk. Using a knife he had in his pocket, he managed to force the lid open. Alas, there was no gold or precious stones in the trunk, all the man found was a machine to print banknotes. Who would have thought that such lies could be perpetrated so long? The banker had never been shipwrecked on the island, he came there voluntarily.

This story sums up very well what happened to our country over the last century, except that the trunk is not on the beach, it just does not exist.

I'd like to think that reading and understanding this story will give you food for thought since it seems very close to today's reality. However, you need to know that the banker is not solely responsible. It is clear that his intention had an obscure goal, but the four men were seduced by the banker's scenario. The banker simply responded to a desire that the four men had in common. The desire to have more... Glory, power and ownership are the only goals sought by people who worship the "Money God". There are many resources on our planet: gold, oil, diamonds, minerals, iron, water, cotton, etc... But only one of these resources is inexhaustible, and whoever owns it has control of the entire planet: this resource is money. Whether metal, paper, scriptural or virtual, it is inexhaustible. So why is there still so much poverty in the world? Because in reducing people to slavery, banks ensure total control of the world. You know the adage: Divide and Conquer?

For some of you, conspiracy theories with the Freemasons and the Illuminati feed your imagination and will sell a lot of books for authors who will fill their pockets, but this kind of reading should be approached with caution and discernment, because it keeps you in a state of confusion and in the role of Victim.

The people who control this planet know that one day the truth will come out in the open, until then, they will strive for maximum profit. Collectively and consciously, if we change our habits now, banks will do as they have always done, that is to say, respond to market demand and adjust to it.

Consequently, we've always had the upper hand, but have ignored it for far too long. Our government is virtually helpless before the power of banks, only the intervention of the community can change our future. That is to say, respond to market demand and adjust the latter. Success will not be gained by violence or war, but by raising our consciousness. We are all responsible for this situation because we feed on false beliefs and desire for power. Later in these pages you will find tools that I hope will help elevate your financial consciousness.

Any value is relative. The twenty-dollar bill you have in your pocket right now does not have a real value. Its value is based solely on the belief you have that this piece of paper will receive the equivalent of its initial value at the time of exchange. In fact, the paper banknote itself is only worth the cost of its production, which is about twenty-seven cents ($0.27). The transaction value is based on the confidence that you assign to it.

Your twenty-dollar bill is actually a promise of future

payment, a bill of exchange. There was a time when our dollar was based on the value of the precious metals in our government's possession. The gold and silver reserves were the wealth of a country. It is not by chance that you will find on the old banknote, the words "Will pay to the bearer the sum of..." Our current banking system no longer rests on the foundation of currency based on metals that our government has in its coffers. Our current financial system is based solely on a credit/debit basis.

Therefore, today's rich international bankers have appropriated themselves the wealth of our country and then they lend it to us with interest. This partly explains the great depression of the thirties, which was caused entirely by rich bankers with inordinate ambitions to have control over the global markets. When the country becomes bankrupt, the creditors (banks) take the opportunity to seize power and the country's assets.

This crisis was perhaps intended to remove the government's power to print money to then give it to a bank so that it can once again lend to the Government with interest. Hence the creation of the central bank that you will find in the majority of the so-called civilized countries of our planet. This merry-go-round was first set up in the United States and shortly after, in Canada and in other countries. The origin of the concept of the central bank comes mainly from England, a small quadrangle called The Square in London. A state in a country enjoying many privileges and run by some very influential families worldwide.

I believe these Englishmen from the Square understood that to build a global empire, one simply needs to manage capital flows. They must control the money supply of all the conquered countries and let them believe that they are sovereign in their legislation and their currency. To do this, you do not need armed men to conquer, you need influential power hungry politicians.

So that the illusion masks the deceit and that the snake is easier to swallow by the Canadian people, we called it the Bank of Canada. The question to ask is whom does the Bank of

Canada lend its money to? Of course, that's right.... the government of Canada. If you look at the Canadian Constitution, which is our supreme law in this country, you will understand that the government has the power to print its own currency. However, following the Great Depression of the 30s, it gave this power to a bank, the Bank of Canada.

Neither you nor I, not even a business can open an account at the Bank of Canada. The Bank of Canada rents banknotes to the government and chartered banks. The fruit of this rental is "interest".

When the interest owed to the bank is too high, it requires the government to raise taxes to pay interest. To ensure the control of the payment of interest, the bank creates the revenue agency that will also act as collection agency to recover all the interest of taxpayers directly through our taxes. Taxes as we know them today appeared shortly after the creation of the central bank to repay the war effort. Moreover you will find the whole history of the creation of the bank and its revenue agency in the minutes and procedures Banking Act 1939: Banking and Commerce in 1939, House of Commons, Standing Committee and Commerce, Minutes of Proceedings and Evidence.

So who owns the Bank of Canada if it doesn't belong to Canadians, you would rightly ask yourself?

CHAPTER 4

THE BANK OF CANADA

In 2004, I met an economist at the Bank of Canada with a journalist who went by the name of Jean-François M., and who was interested in my research on the banking sector. First, I learned that a citizen does not have the right to meet an economist at the Central Bank. Then I had to answer a questionnaire, which asked me about my religious beliefs and my political interests. I then spoke with a lady from the Bank who assessed me on the phone and whom I fortunately managed to persuade that I was harmless. She told me that I could accompany the journalist, but I had no right to ask questions.

In addition, the meeting would be outside the bank building in an AL Van Houtte Café on McGill College Avenue. The conversation was to be recorded by the economist, but we would not have the right to a copy.

During the meeting, I took the opportunity to look really innocent, the economist had no clue that I had questions for him. The reporter asked him a few questions to flatter his ego when suddenly the batteries from the economists' tape recorder went dead. Sometimes synchronicity falls just right. So the reporter asked the following question: "Is the Bank of Canada a private bank?" The economist explained that the bank belonged to Canadians and that the Minister of Finance held 100 % of the shares and blah, blah, blah...

At the time of our meeting, the economist had taken care to give us a booklet explaining the history and the budgets of the bank. With a slightly sarcastic expression, I raised my hand and I asked him for the first time if I could ask him a question. Seeing the opportunity to flee the reporter's question and thinking to wash his hands of it, he turned to me with a big smile and said:

"Sure ... what is your question? And I asked him:

> *When the Bank of Canada makes a decision on the budget or monetary policy, is the decision that is made in a national or global interest?*

He replied:

> Decisions are taken in the common interest to protect the interests and integrity of all central banks

> *Uh, can I ask another question, sir? Does the Bank of Canada have to report its activities to another bank for the benefit of all?*
> Of course, he replied.

> *And what is this bank?* I asked.
> This is the B.I.S. (Bank of International Settlement), he said..

> *So if I understand correctly, decisions are made in a global rather than national interest?* I said, summarizing his remarks.
> Uh, yes that would be correct.

> *Is it also correct that the Minister of Finance possesses 100% of shares without a voting right? As I believe is written right there in your little booklet...*
> Yes, that's right, he said, now frowning.

> *Sir, if decisions are taken in a global interest, if our minister has no power and the bank serves interests other than those of Canadians ... it's called a private bank?* I added..
> Uh, I do not have the right to respond to that question, as it pertains to bank secrecy sir!" he said dryly.

To allow him to regain control of the conversation, I opened the booklet he gave us and I asked him to explain how budgets work. He proceeds to reveal his great economist theories and begins to explain the budget with major academic words I can barely understand. Then suddenly I see the big hole and I ask him if I can ask another question. He unsuspectingly accepts, once again believing he masters his field.

> *Sir, it says here in your booklet that there is 45 billion dollars in paper money and currency in circulation, is that correct¿*
> "Yes that's right!" he replies.

> *Sir, it is written here that with the scriptural money in the bank accounts, all together the two combined totals 100 billion in circulation, is that correct¿*
> Exactly, it's written right there, he said.

> *So how can we possibly repay a debt of 660 billion with only $100 billion in circulation¿ It is mathematically impossible! This is the scam of the century!*
> Ah! Indeed, it is a mystery that I had not noticed, but this is not a scam, it's something else ...he replied embarrassed.

> *It's something else¿ Then by all means do explain!*
> Oh no. That's Bank secrecy! he said, hoping to end the interview.

I dared to ask him if I could ask another question. He agreed, but was very suspicious this time around.

> *Sir, is it true that our government borrows on the head of its citizens in the amount of $850,000 at the moment of each individuals birth and that these individuals will repay this amount through the payment of taxes throughout their lives¿*
> No, this is not how it is done! he says.

There was a moment of silence.

> *Is that Bank secrecy¿* I said.
> Yes, he said.

> *Does the Government then, sell its accounts to the Bank of Canada to get loans in return, as is done in the private sector¿ Is it through Statistics Canada, that taxpayers are assessed as*

an asset on the books according to their status and their future wages and taxes receivable are payable to the Government as an advance loan?

You know what his answer was? Guess? It was the last question. He rose, grabbed his coat and left in a hurry.

The Bank of Canada today, is and always has been based on the model of a private company, that is to say, constituting of a capital of five million dollars divided into one hundred thousand shares with a nominal value of fifty dollars each. It was in 1938[9] that the shares of the Bank of Canada were purchased by the Minister of Finance who holds them on behalf of the Government of Canada. These shares represent the Minister of Finances ownership of the assets of the Bank of Canada. A large part of the assets of the Bank consists of its investment portfolio, which is mostly composed of government securities.

Subsequently, the income the Bank of Canada receives from this portfolio minus its operating expenses is paid to the Canadian government, which by means of the Minister of finance is the owner. In 2003, these payments totalled more than $ 1.8 billion.

Today, 60 % of the world population produces 100 % of global goods, even if 20 % of them hold 80 %.[10] How is this possible knowing that the only currency exchange (exchangeable wealth) is the labour force and natural resources? In reading these facts, we are entitled to ask ourselves about the real value of what we call in unison "money." When I speak of real value, I mean a currency supported by a gold equivalent, clothing, tools, furniture, etc... But in fact, is the currency in Canada, still guaranteed with an equivalent of gold?

---

9   From it's opening in March 1935 until 1938, the Bank of Canada is a private institution.
10 www.banquemondiale.org.

CHAPTER 5

THE BANKRUPTCY OF 1933

I t is on June 5th in 1933 that President Roosevelt approved and passed resolution 192 (House of Joint Resolution - HJR-192 or 192) which suspended the convertibility of gold into any negotiable instrument (paper money, bonds, etc..). This resolution occurred almost three months to the day, after the President's 2039 proclamation, known as the Bank Holiday, suspending due to national emergency and in accordance with chapter 12, article 95(b) of the United States Code, from Monday March 6th 1933 to Thursday March 9th 1933 inclusively, all banking activities across the United States.

The United States (like Canada) following the adoption of this Resolution fell once more in their history, into bankruptcy: *"All the people reading this know how it all went down in 1914, we were then bankrupt, just like today.* [11]*"* In this case bankruptcy meaning *"lack of legal money (gold) to cover banknotes put into circulation."* At that time, the modern goldsmiths had ostensibly issued more receipts or guarantee bonds than the amount of gold in the reserve.

The establishment of a central bank in Canada. Following the U.S. and Canadian economic mess, and following the adoption on March 30th of 1933, the motion that authorized the

---

11   Bank and commerce. Journal of the House of Commons.

Governor in Council to suspend the redemption of Dominion notes (converted into gold), it is officially on April 10th 1933, by decree of the Council, that the suspension of convertibility of Dominion notes against gold took place in Canada. Since 1935, the Canadian dollar is no longer backed by gold:

"The Bank is required to redeem the notes payable on demand to the bearer that were outstanding March 11, 1935 and before that" date constituted a direct obligation of Canada; these banknotes continue to be legal tender. [12] "

In turn, the Canadian dollar became the target of speculators of all kinds, which was not without influence on exchange rates. From a fixed exchange rate based on gold, the dollar now went to a floating exchange rate, in other words unstable. It is this instability of the value of the Canadian dollar that particularly motivated the Canadian government to establish a commission, July of 1933. The commission's mandate was to review the operation of the Finance Act and the usefulness of establishing a central bank institution in Canada with a primary mandate to regulate the value of the Canadian dollar.

Seven weeks after the start of public hearings, members of the Committee and its Chairman, handed over the final report to the Government supporting the establishment of a central bank in Canada (Bank of Canada).

It is by majority decision that the committee recommended the establishment of a central bank for Canada, and according to the council should also have a dual purpose: "Within the limits imposed by law and by its ability, endeavour to regulate credit and currency in safeguarding the best interests of the economic life of the nation and control and defend, in its capacity, the external value of the national currency unit"and as second objective: "Seek to mitigate by its influence fluctuations in the general level of economic activity as it falls within the area of monetary policy." [13]

---

12   The Bank of Canada Act S.R., c. B-2, Article 1. It should be noted that these Dominion Banknotes were on rare occasions fully secured by a sum in gold
13   The Privacy Committee , Royal Bank and Currency Commission, July 31, 1933

The Bank of Canada opened its doors on March 11th, 1935, after receiving Royal Assent on July 3rd, 1934. It was this same year that the Law on the Bank of Canada Act replaced the law on the Dominion bank notes and the Finance Act. The Bank of Canada today, under Article 25

(1) of the Act on the Bank of Canada, is the only institution empowered to issue bank notes. Not the only institution to create "money", but the only institution to print paper money as legal tender. The distinction is important.

Banknotes VS scriptural currency. Let us first of all make the distinction between two types of currency: paper money (printed by the Bank of Canada and now totalling about 40 billion dollars) and scriptural currency, that is to say, consisting solely of digits in a computer which is also called bank credit.

In figures, this gives present day Canada a total money supply of about 800 billion of which $ 40 billion is paper currency issued by the Bank of Canada, that is to say 5 % of all Canadian money in circulation. So who has the power to create money, the government or the private sector?

In this regard, Mr. Slaght, during a debate in the House of Commons on May 15th, 1939: " *... Parliament has delegated this power [to issue currency] to the Bank of Canada.* "

However, section 91 of the Canadian Constitution, the supreme law of the land, gives Parliament exclusive authority over money, the mintage and the interest on the money, controlled since 1934 by the Bank of Canada (remember that the Bank of Canada is a corporation, agent of the Government of Canada [14], but that the decisions taken are solely made by the steering committee, and not the Minister of Finance who has no right to vote; "Advisory capacity" under the Bank of Canada Act, so it is said, to separate the power to print money from the power to spend it). Parliament does not have a veto over the actions and decisions taken by the Bank of Canada, it is

---

14   Even if the Bank is working for the Canadian government, it is a separate entity

questionable whether this institution is not unconstitutional [15].

Prior to 1991, chartered banks had to retain a minimum of banknotes from the Bank of Canada in their reserves for the right to create credit.

Afterwards and with Bill C-46, the necessary reserves were reduced to 0 %. Banks therefore have the power to create money from nothing " ... the banker is thus allowed to create a currency substitute, lend it as if it were money and require not only the interest, but the reimbursement of the interest and the capital in currency, loans that are nothing more than entries on the account books. "As a result, the community is still in debt to the bank for more money than the bank actually issued, because the bank never issues the interest money the community is obligated to pay[16]. "

Reserves of 0 %. On June 17th, 1999, Bill C-84 passed by the House of Commons simply repealed section 457 of the Bank Act, the article made mention of the reserves needed by chartered banks, constituted in harmony with this law should maintain for the granting of the credit. Contrariwise, in 2006, the BIS [17] (Bank of International Settlement)[18], the central bank of all central banks, could require that all banks prove reserves of at least 25 % to support the creation of money. (Confirmed by Mr. David Dupuis, economist at the Bank of Canada).

Nowadays, no reserve is required under Canadian law on the creation of money by banks: *"If all our depositors had, as did those of the United States, claimed their deposits, all of Canada's banks would have gone bankrupt. [...] We are insolvent nationally as well as internationally[19] "*

At present, chartered banks grant on average twenty-five

---

15   Under Article 91 of the Canadian Constitution, the banks, the incorporation of banks, the issue of paper currency and interest on money are areas which Parliament has exclusive legislative authority.

16   M.G.G. McGeer, Banking and Commerce, Journals of the House of Commons, 1934, p. 516. Task

17   was before that date, the responsibility of the chartered banks.

18   www.bis.org.

19   Ibid., M.G.G. McGeer, p. 526.

times more credit than they have in reserve [20]. For every dollar deposited in their coffers, the Government of Canada, through the Bank Act of Canada, allows them to lend twenty-five dollars at interest rates determined by the private sector. This practice is called money fractionation. After reading this information I attributed the nickname "Bank-aire" system to the present monetary system. Unfortunately, it is a French pun and is not really translatable, but for the sake of this transcript I will give you a quick breakdown anyway. The French word "banquaire" meaning "banking" breaks down into two words "banque = bank" and "aire=air".

It was probably the shady banking practices that persuaded MGG McGeer to say in the 1934 Journals of the House of Commons: *"In view of our actions, instead of being proud of being public men we should be surprised that the public lets us live."*

Later, he adds: "There is no reason, in our system, for mercantile banks not to continue to do what they have done so far, that being, to serve the private interests. But when it comes to allowing a private banker to seize public credit and administer it in his favour as a monopoly, it is time that all public men oversee this, because under the system in which we now live, we rent our nations' public credit to a financial group who administers it with two goals in mind: first the private interest of monopoly, and second maintaining the purchasing power of the consumer and supporting the taxpayer's ability to pay. Unfortunately, however, the latter has been greatly neglected. So neglected in fact, that from one end to the other of the Dominion, municipal, provincial and national bankruptcy, are apparent everywhere ..."

In most cases, chartered banks only lend money they have in their coffers, but they give payment promises that are honoured on the financial market. Duncan Cameron and Ed Finn explain in "Top 10 myths about the Canadian deficit":

"Banks create money whenever they decide to grant a new loan. Borrowers promise the bank to repay the loan with

---

20   All the money currently in circulation in the form of paper money with legal tender issued by The Bank of Canada represents only $ 42 billion, or about 5% of the total money supply (which borders 800 billion.)

interest at a specified time and the banks, in turn, promise to pay the amount borrowed from the signing of the agreement. The money supply increases with the amount of each loan. Of course, the money supply decreases the amount of capital, when the loan is fully repaid."

The word **capital** is very important since it is not the total amount (capital + interest) which decreases the money supply once the amount is fully repaid, interest is added to the money by not having created any wealth to support the value.

The Bank of Canada, fully public? Although shares of the Bank reside in the hands of the Government of Canada, its management remains private (if you look in the phone book to find the phone numbers of the Bank of Canada, you will have to look in the business section, and not under the government blue pages, through the Executive Committee consisting of the Governor (now David Dodge), Deputy Governor and two to four directors selected by the Board. The Deputy Minister of Finance - or the person replacing him- sits on the steering committee, but as I mentioned earlier, in an advisory capacity only, that is to say, without the right to vote.

The creation of Canadian currency to fund Canada's debt will inevitably have the effect of moving the collective wealth to private interests for the greater satisfaction thereof. We must not forget that every time we make a loan, we transfer a property right. Our ongoing borrowing results in the increased ownership of a certain class of the population at the expense of property rights of the whole nation, so that today a large proportion of the wealth of this country is owned by a small percentage of the Canadian population.

Moreover, as we shall see later, this method of money creation from banks creates a huge need to control inflation, including taxation and income taxes: "They - the municipalities, provinces, governments - cooperate to regulate currency circulation, but they do not tax to maintain the government, they tax to prevent inflation. [21]"

As the ironic saying goes, nowadays it seems more profitable to open a financial institution than to rob one.

The news from the past decade has enabled us to open our eyes to several questionable practices, through the actions of Mr. Yves Michaud [22], who defended small shareholders tooth and nail. Rightfully nicknamed "Robin Hood of Banks". One needs to read his works to understand the extent of protectionism and obscurity of this wealthy mafia.

---

21 *Ibid.,* p.538
22 http://fr.wikipedia.org/wiki/Yves_Michaud;
Read the following book : Michaud, Yves, The reasons for anger, Fides, 2005 or see http://www.livresquebecois.com/livre.asp?id=bwisdugbwabpe&/les-raisons-de-la-colere/yves-michaud

CHAPTER 6

THE 2007 to 2015 FINANCIAL CRISIS

When an economy is experiencing a recession, the central bank and the government adopt fiscal (tax cuts and mail-out remittance checks to citizens) and expansionary monetary policies (interest rate cuts) to get by. Normally these tools are enough to revive the economy as has been demonstrated in the past during recessions (1987-1991, and many others later). Once these expansionary policies are in place, it takes about nine months before the economy starts to feel the benefits. (Low interest rates encourage consumption and investment, and therefore economic recovery).

These are the first steps taken by central banks and governments. This is what the United States, Europe and other countries did in early fall 2007 to address the crisis that began in August 2007. They brought their interest rates down several times and mailed checks out from September 2007 to April 2008. So, logically, the global economy should respond positively to these expansionary policies in the late summer - early autumn 2008 if it is based on the nine months that it normally takes for the economy to improve in these rate cuts. But as we can see, this is not the case, as the crisis, on the contrary, has expanded. Why?

Essentially, it was not an economic crisis (i.e. recession) that the world experienced in August 2007, but a financial crisis. The magnitude of the financial crisis could not be contained since the fall of 2007, which consequently led the world into a severe economic crisis. How serious? **Recession or Depression?**

It is now known that the expansionary policies since autumn 2007 have not helped us (so it mustn't be a recession). The economy has been declining and we see lower prices (around 60 %) of all tangible assets (real estate, natural resources, oil-metals) and financial (stocks, bonds). At least that was the case until 2010. They're not just speaking of recession or depression now, but of deflation as well (falling prices). What should central banks and governments do to combat deflation? That is the question, because when the economy is in a period of inflation (rising prices), the central bank has to raise interest rates to slow spending for consumption and investment as was the case in the 80s (ex. in 1980-81, the inflation rate was about 13 % and mortgage rates were 20 %). But when there is deflation, the strategy should be the opposite, that is to say lower rates.

This is what the International Monetary Fund asked at the meeting of G-20 in the Summer-Fall of 2008. Like me, since then, you've observed that almost all other industrialized countries and their rates have fallen sharply and show to this date an interest rate of almost ZERO (something never-seen). When this concerted effort by central banks is not enough to revive the economy and get us out of deflation, an alternative is quantitative easing (QE). The only central bank that has experienced this approach to overcome deflation is the one in Japan in March 2001.

The principle of QE is to reduce the rate to almost zero (which the global central banks have done since the fall of 2007) and inject liquidity into the banking system (again, this practice is today applied in several countries). Now that the rate is almost zero and the governments will continue to support the banking system with massive liquidity injections (it would not be surprising to see in the coming months nationalization of the largest banks): how are they going to contain the rampant deflation across the planet?

To counter deflation, governments and central banks will do everything to RE-INFLATE the economy (raising prices). After dropping interest rates, mailing checks to citizens, reducing individual and corporate taxes, trying to save the banking system, they will engage in exorbitant spending on infrastructure. I'm not teaching you anything, you have only to look at the zillions of dollars in initiatives undertaken by the United States, China, Europe and others in 2009.

Will all these bailouts succeed in overcoming deflation? The experience of QE to constrain the deflation in Japan in the early 2000s shows otherwise. Some would argue that the Bank of Japan was too slow to respond to the phenomenon of deflation which has ravaged (and in my opinion, continues to undermine) Japan since the late 80s. We must remember that Japan was the largest economy of the 70s. This prosperity created a speculative bubble in Japan in the stock and property markets in the 80's, which deflated and caused deflation. Just as the speculative bubble in real estate in the United States since 2002 and the debt that it necessitated, the real estate markets collapsed in 2007.

But it would seem that we, Americans and Europeans were more astute than the Japanese in 2009 and that we responded with caution and sped up the plague of deflation ... ... It remains to be seen. I believe there is NOTHING that central banks and governments can do to get rid of deflation. This plague must follow its normal course and it is only through debt write-off by the bankruptcy of some banks, corporations and individuals, that the economy will renew itself. This purge can take 10 to 15 years if we base ourselves on the experience of the Great Depression of the 30's. The debt level of all stakeholders (governments, corporations and individuals) is beyond the capacity of the economy to serve the debt. The economic downturn slows bank profits, corporations and individuals and reduces their ability to repay interest and capital debt.

Supposing I am wrong and that the QE accomplishes what it is supposed to do, that is to say RE-INFLATE the economy. The assumption is that these injections of liquidity into the system will increase the economic recovery through job creation. The more people work, the more consumption increases and inevitably causes pressure for prices to go up. The price increase is the secret to overcoming the deflation that causes havoc on prices. But if liquidity creation (by the central bank) is greater than economic growth (Gross Domestic Product), this will lead to inflation. Based on the amount of money being (and in the future) put out into circulation worldwide by central banks, it will not be surprising to see in the next 12 to 18 months, a fairly dramatic increase in inflation. So, to solve the plague of deflation, there is a new problem created, which is the risk of hyperinflation, because there is too much money chasing after a small amount of goods and services.

For an investor, what are the possibilities in an inflationary environment? Contrary to deflation, when inflation is climbing they want to hold onto tangible assets such as buildings, metals, oil, natural gas, etc.., But especially precious metals such as gold, silver and platinum.

As the government hates deflation, it will put measures in place to fight it, and it will be the same if inflation exceeds the allowable range. Certainly in the short term, the government will accept a rate above this range to ensure that the price increase is indeed rooted in the economic system, but if inflation continues its pace, the government will soon implement restrictive monetary and fiscal policies. It would not be surprising, within 24 to 36 months to see a rise in interest rates and possibly tax increases. In order to get us out of deflation, the debts incurred by the government need to be repaid.

The question remains: are we heading towards another Great Depression (because the inability to counter deflation will inevitably precipitate us into depression), or the almost unquantifiable amount of money creation to RE-INFLATE the economy will eventually lead us to hyperinflation? Some argue that the Great Depression of the 30's could have been minimized if the policies of President Hoover had not been so harsh.

He applied restrictive monetary and fiscal policies (he raised the interest rate in 1929-1930 and taxes in 1930 to balance his budget) instead of expansionary policies that the United States, Europe, Canada and other countries have recently favoured. But again, are these interventions the miracle recipe to macro-economic problems?

History shows that the economy and its stakeholders in the private sector are better equipped for more effective and efficient resource redistribution. Also, maybe these economic macro cycles are part of the capitalist system that we must live with? A Russian economist developed a theory, the Kondratieff cycle to try to explain the causes of the Great Depression of the 30's. According to him, the economy is operating on cycles of 60 years within which there are several cycles (3-5 years) recessions/recoveries, mainly caused by inventory adjustments of the world production machine.

His theory can be verified if you consider that depressions occurred at intervals of about 60 years (the depression of 1873 and 1930/1945) and considering the current crisis that began in 2007, which gives between 55-60 years since the end of the last depression. Is it just a coincidence or is his theory verifiable?

Many economists agree that the most important monetary crash will take place between 2012 and 2015. In short, all the theories here are feasible, as they are virtually all possible. It is clear that our current economic system is a monumental failure, given the current technology and human consciousness. It is unthinkable today that humans do not have drinking water, nothing to eat and no habitat. It is a crime against humanity and in my humble opinion, the current monetary system based on the globalization of poverty must change. And this, without further due notice or delay, as bank lawyers would say!

I am not alone in thinking so; others firmly believe that all this must change.

For all these reasons, it is high time to act and take back our power. I believe, as stated repeatedly by professor Léo-Paul

Lauzon, from the Department of Accounting Studies and Chair of socio-economic study of UQAM, that the banks should be nationalized and their billions of profits redistributed to the community.

CHAPTER 7

THE ORIGIN OF CREDIT

Throughout history, from ancient times to today, credit has existed in many forms. The scarcity of currency and the dollar (being circulated in controlled quantity by the government or the banks to keep the value of their currency) led to the emergence of credit. In the dictionary, the meaning of credit includes two definitions: It can mean the ability of a person to obtain goods or services before payment, based on the trust that payment will be made in the future. It also refers to reputation "enjoys high credibility or a large influence".

We can also speak of "credit" as a promise of future payment or the delay necessary for a person to acquire property or a possession because they do not have the money to buy it now and will reimburse it later.

In ancient times, credit was granted only to military commanders or monarchies through "exchange-traded notes". These letters were often called "letters of credit." This type of letter of credit was popular at the time of the Crusaders. Templar Knights whose mission was to accompany the pilgrims on their journey to the Holy Land carried a bill of exchange, which was then cashed in by the Templar Commanders in Jerusalem. Thus, the robbers could no longer capture the poor people and rob them of their gold coins during the trip between their country and the Holy Land.

The Order of the Templar or commonly called the Poor Knights of Christ was an important pre-banking treasury organization at the time. Their knights were warrior monks who took vows of poverty and chastity. They were known as men of good and justice; seigniories were granted to some of them for the purpose of maintaining fertile lands and prosperous villagers. All the knight's possessions were bequeathed to the order during his induction into the temple. A knight was in the service of the Order and therefore could not acquire property. As a servant of God, the knight's desire to love and serve was a higher and more honorable calling than his desire for fame, power and wealth. In the span of three hundred years, the Templars and the Templar Knights accumulated a colossal fortune.

They even loaned large sums to the monarchy of the time. The Order made loans without interest to pilgrims with landholding for their pilgrimage, and once back, they enjoyed the usufruct of the harvest and became somehow the managers of the land, yet benefited 100 % of the yield. Land therefore became the property of the Order as if they had bought it. The pilgrim left with his credit letter and could cash the sum he needed in the Templar commanderies on the road to Jerusalem. Today, in our modern society, we call this type of loan a "mortgage." Except we pay interest on the loan.

Certainly, if the King of France in 1307, Philippe le Bel had not conspired to kill all the Templar Knights by burning them at the stake and take the opportunity to steal all the gold in the commanderies for personal gain, could the world today have possibly had a more prosperous economy, without poverty?

Poor King Philippe could never get hold of the treasure of the Templars, because all the gold had mysteriously disappeared. Furthermore, he died shortly afterwards in mysterious ways. Hence the famous superstition of Friday, October 13, 1307 related to the curse of the Templars against the king and his descendants, pronounced by the Master of the Order Jacques de Molay, a few seconds before dying at the stake.

Later on, during the Age of Discovery, monarchies perpetuated the system of exchange notes used by the Templar Knights.

For example, when the King of France sent ships to New France to import or export goods, one ship out of three sank on the high seas with a cargo full of gold. This, of course, was very costly to the king, hence the importance of exchange notes payable to the bearer. Our current system of credit is still based on the same grounds, the exchange note or commonly called "promissory note or notes" has been replaced by the green paper bills we have in our pocket today. Checks, bank drafts and money orders are actually the same as exchange notes.

Then, early in the century, in small villages, another form of credit bureaus emerged. It was known as the general store, where people went to learn all about the lives of everyone. The shopkeeper knew almost everything about the financial situation of the inhabitants of his village. He gave credit and even gave out loans. The village priest was also a good source of information on some parishioners, but he was bound by his faith in secrecy.

In a banking system where loans are made to individuals, it is important to minimize the risk of delinquency to maximize profits. People believe that the bank lends the money of depositors and investors. This is not exactly the way money is created in a bank. It is actually created from the fractionation. The income of the bank, it is not money that banks create, but the interest they generate. You can find more information about it by reading the chapter on it in the book about the banks and the Standing Committee on Banking and Commerce in 1939 in very limited copies in used book stores, stored with dusty books left behind by our law students. This approach continues to create money ever since.

This idea of fractionation came from European goldsmiths who regularly changed exchange notes into to gold for farmers. It is the Bauer family of goldsmiths, later known as the Rothschild family, which seems to be the author of this curious ploy. They found that only one farmer in ten returned for the gold he had given on deposit with the goldsmith. Farmers preferred to share the credit notes among themselves rather than return for gold. Hence the idea of creating banknotes. The goldsmith issued more credit notes than gold he possessed in his coffers. Thus, transaction costs and interest were lucrative for him and people could transact safely without being robbed of their gold coins. But at what price? This merry-go-round of banking fractionation continues since that period. Some will tell you today, it is 25 times the deposits which are lent in short, ask your bank manager, because only he knows the answer.

The appearance of credit agencies. In the 70s and 80s, credit bureaus made their appearance at the request of banks. Certain credit rating agencies emerged in Canada. Then, several agencies were bought by their competitors to finally become two major ones known today under the names of Equifax and Groupecho (TransUnion). Credit information was exchanged by telephone between banks and credit bureaus, then in the 90's, the fax machine appeared. Equifax was formerly called the Montreal Credit Bureau.

With the advent of the Internet, the speed at which information can be transmitted has greatly contributed to improving the management and exchange of information.

For the average person, lets forget the idea that credit information agencies only exist to ensure the safe collection of our financial information. These agencies are not government agencies and they do not create our credit record for our benefit. Their purpose is not to ensure that our credit information is true and accurate, and they will not send us an annual copy of our credit report.

Agencies are something far different from what most people believe. To put it simply, these agencies are companies that make money selling our information. They sell our information to creditors, employers, insurance companies, advertising agencies ... and even ourselves! They are in fact private companies, just like the corner store.

The two major agencies in Canada, Equifax and TransUnion, were originally small local survey companies. These agencies will accumulate all the information they consider relevant to us, including our employment history, our marital status, our age, our credit history and in certain cases, even our race, our religion and all other information they can find about us. They subsequently sell this information to creditors who will use it to determine whether they should give us credit or not, and if so, at what interest rate.

Over time, these agencies became so powerful that they had to be regulated to protect us in the face of this power. This led to the Fair Credit Reporting Act (FCRA), which was passed ... in the United States! Nothing, or very little, exists in Canada, to protect us against this encroachment of our personal information. The Office of the Information Commissioner is the provincial agency, which has jurisdiction over suppression or correction of personal information found incorrect or misleading. Unfortunately, processing times are very long and the commissioners do not seem to understand the workings of this very complicated system.

Credit scoring has become extremely important and it is the agencies that have total control of the information used to create this score. The problem is that the purpose of these agencies is to collect our information and sell it. This means that even if these agencies are the only absolute source of our information, they have no incentive to ensure that the information they hold about us is complete and accurate. They accumulate the information they find as well as that given to them, add it to our file, and sell it! And creditors assume that this information is true and accurate.

In 2006, we were able to get our hands on the contract that the Equifax members sign. Pay attention to the underlined text and you will understand very quickly that they do not care about the validity of the information transmitted to them.

CONTRACT

This agreement occurring on_____
between Equifax Canada inc., a Canadian company
(*hereinafter called Equifax*)
and _____ (*Member*).

Considering the mutual commitments and agreements involved in this, the parties agree as follows:

1. The member will provide Equifax, without fee to Equifax, regularly every _____ days, all tapes, in mutually convenient form , or other media containing credit transactions, current and updated (hereinafter called "information"), of the member's customers. The member will bear the costs of preparation and delivery of these tapes or other media for Equifax. Equifax, at its own expense, will incorporate information from magnetic tapes or other media, computerized reporting system Equifax credit, but not incorporate such information so as to create in any way whatsoever a client segregation from the member. The information thus added will become the exclusive property of Equifax magnetic tapes and other media delivered to Equifax under this Agreement shall remain the property of the member and will be promptly returned, once Equifax has completed the process of reproduction and will have added information to the computerized credit records system.

2. Equifax can transmit or provide to any party using its services credit records and who has signed an agreement, the services permitted under the law and in accordance with the normal use of the Equifax database.

3. The member must make every possible effort to provide Equifax with accurate and reliable credit information, however, the member does not guarantee the accuracy or completeness of such information. Neither the member nor its officers, employees or representatives shall be liable to Equifax, for any claim or damage, and any damage suffered by Equifax, following the transmission of this information to Equifax credit.

4. Equifax will defend, indemnify and hold the member harmless for any costs and liabilities whatsoever, which may be attributed to the member as a result of misuse by Equifax, the credit information provided to Equifax by the member, provided that the member shall immediately notify Equifax in writing, of any claim submitted to them, or any legal proceedings brought against the member, which, according to the member, are subject to the foregoing and are entitled to protection, compensation and recognition of non-responsibility.

Such notices shall be addressed as follows:

President
Equifax Canada Inc.

Credit Information Services
110, Sheppard Avenue East
Toronto (Ontario)
M2N 6S1

5. This agreement shall continue in force for a period of twelve months from the date of commencement of the Contract and automatically renew itself from year to year. However, Equifax or the member may terminate the agreement by giving 30 days written notice to the other party.

6. This agreement is evidence of the entire agreement relating to the subject matter, between Equifax and the member, and supersedes all prior agreements or representations made oral or written. It can only be modified by an agreement in writing, duly signed by the authorized representatives of Equifax and the member.

IN WITNESS WHEREOF, Equifax and the member agreed that this agreement is signed by their duly authorized representatives, the date specified above.

NAME OF THE BUSINESS: _____

By: _____

EQUIFAX CANADA INC.: _____

By: _____

So, it is your responsibility to ensure that the information appearing on your credit report is up to date and accurate. Unfortunately, when you want to make a correction, Equifax is not that cooperative. In a later chapter you will find the steps to take to change incorrect information.

Your file is created on the first day you make your very first request for credit from a financial institution. Depending on when the institution applies for a report, the latter is instantly created in the system of the agency consulted by your financial institution.

Afterwards, with each new credit application you make, all the new information will be added to update your credit report for future reference. At Equifax, the majority of information will be purged from the system after six (6) years in the case of TransUnion however, it will stay "ad vitam aeternam" (eternally) accessible to the creditor.

The main purpose of these companies is to keep up to date and make available information on the state of your personal finances.

It's the members of the credit bureaus that send monthly information to keep their records up to date. Some institutions do this every 30 days, others every 60 days and sometimes 90 days. Because updates are not made regularly, the clients credit score is thus vulnerable to inaccuracies and the current record could have errors.

Among the members, there are credit unions and banks,

finance companies, leasing companies, credit card companies, service providers and retailers (merchants).

For example, your financial institution may report to the credit bureau that you occasionally pay your loan a few days late.

Similarly, the institution that financed credit to a consumer for a purchase such as a home theater through a merchant can transmit to a credit reporting agency information that you have not made your final payment.

What allows these agencies to keep the information records on a client, is the client's consent, previously obtained by the financial institution in a contractual agreement.

There is no legal relationship between the consumer and the credit agencies and this is the main reason why it is so difficult to contact them for any assistance. For these superpowers of information, you're just a commodity. They have little interest in your rights and your reputation.

But there is a contract between financial institutions and the credit agencies.

The two parties agree to exchange information that is said to be up to date and accurate. This is what makes the entire system of approval of financial institutions supposedly impervious and reliable.

We now have the right to obtain a free copy of our file and we have the right to challenge the veracity and accuracy of the information found therein. This does not mean that agencies are now ensuring the accuracy of the information they hold and they sell. It only means that we can challenge the information.

Unfortunately, this trend has not eradicated all the problems of this system. These credit agencies remain huge businesses with enormous power. They are motivated primarily by money they collect from selling the contents of our file.

Agencies cannot refuse the right of consumers to challenge the information they hold. But we are entitled to ask whether it would not be profitable for all parties to promote a negative track record to the consumer.

Thus, the agencies do what they can to prevent us from challenging the information they hold and they sell. The alleged motivation of these agencies to discourage consumers and to maintain derogatory information (ie: of negative character) could be to affect the credit score for consumption. This fictitious approach would increase the risk of consumer delinquency.

They are judge and jury to decide whether information that is on your record is true or not. In short, for the moment, it is they who decide arbitrarily and do not give you any right of appeal or revision.

They will not tell you which body to contact to correct the information. Probably having no other choice, you could acquiesce as the majority of people do or turn to a law firm and pay huge fees to correct an error that you didn't make yours. What they ultimately want, is for you to be discouraged in undertaking expensive procedures, so that you will give up and just let it go.

The civil lawyers know very little about the field of credit bureaus. In general, they are dismissed before the court as banks prefer to hire firms with experienced lawyers who have a ton of arguments and a limitless budget to confuse the opposing party and stretch the gravy to the max. Meanwhile the debtor is exhausted and abandons all procedures.

However, there are solutions available with the information access Commission that has jurisdiction in these matters. Unfortunately, you won't learn this information from the credit bureaus.

What is a Credit Report? A credit report is a standardized portrait of a person's financial behaviour. It is also in some regard a photograph of the consumer's financial situation. As we have explained above, it is by exercising your consent that the information is exchanged between a financial institution and a credit agency. The virtual picture of your behaviour as a customer identifies and compiles information about you, which serves to assess you in terms of potential risk.

When you request a copy of your credit report from these agencies, the latter send you a detailed copy of your record, explaining this and that and all their privacy policies as well as detailed explanations of your record. However, for many consumers not familiar with the functioning of consumer credit, the understanding of a credit report remains a jargon that only bankers and industry professionals can understand. Fortunately, in recent years, agencies have improved the version given to consumers, they explain a little better what is meant by the information found on their records.

When financial institutions access your credit report, they consult it in a different format from yours, one that is much easier to read and interpret. However, in their agreement, agencies formally prohibit the financial institution to relinquish you a copy. Yet, it is your file, isn't it? This refusal is probably related to grounds for prosecution. As this type of record is easier to read, consumers could detect more easily what causes discrimination in their credit report.

A recent study of the issue on the French Canadian TV show "La Facture" (a show that assists consumers in finding out the truth) showed that 80 % of credit reports contained errors and that in 90 % of cases, it was detrimental to the consumer. Hence forth, when you ask to be mailed a copy of your credit report, either from Equifax or TransUnion, you will receive a form to update your credit file.

You must carefully check each piece of information reported therein and request a correction if necessary, via the update form. You can easily correct certain information such as address, the city, postal code, an error in your name, information about your employer or previous employers and any information registered about you. However, it will be difficult to modify disputed information pertaining to an account. This is where things get complicated. You find yourself before an administrative dinosaur that cares little for the prejudice that such an error may cause you. Following your request for an update regarding an account that has an error, it is common for the consumer to be faced with a resounding "no" with no possibility of an appeal.

Before going further, there are important aspects that you need to understand about the current financial system. Through this book, you will discover a different vision of our debit/credit banking system. You are called, as a person, to play a role, a character. Knowing that you play a character in this great theatrical play we call "society", it will now be easier to play the game of Monopoly that is this emotionless society. Now you know that in any event everything you possess in this country does not belong to the human being that you are, but to the character that you represent. So what good is it to want to own property if it doesn't really belong to you?

You ask yourself: So my house, is it mine? My car? The answer is no! Stop paying your property taxes and you will quickly see who owns the house. You do not possess the title to actual property, you own a lot determined by a certificate of location. In Canada, the land belongs to the government and it sells you a right to use it through the Regional County Municipality (RCM) and municipalities.

To understand the present and prepare for our future, we must know the past. Unfortunately, our textbooks have failed to educate us about the functioning of our capitalist banking system. Today, with both feet firmly rooted in the biggest financial crisis in decades, we find that we are facing doom and impoverishment of the middle class system, as well as global monopoly by the banks.

So, in closing this chapter, you now know that it is possible to move from the stand-in to the actor, and from actor to master of his destiny through increased awareness, in order to act this play brilliantly, in a role other than the eternal debtor. Your credit record deserves a review? There are courses to help you draw a portrait of your situation realistically and establish your recovery budget.

IN CONCLUSION...

The time has come for everyone to take stock of their financial situation. In the back of your mind, try to get a picture of what your relationship is with money.

1 Are you negative about money?

2 Does lack of money prevent you from realizing your goals?

3 Are you in the habit of making a budget?

4 Despite your efforts, are you still financially insecure?

5 Does talking about money make you feel uncomfortable? Why?

Take a step back to see more clearly. Many people have negative feelings toward money dating back to their childhood, often from a difficult start in life.

- Before I was 10 years old: How did I use my first savings?

- Between 10 and 15 years: was my pocket money sufficient for my needs?

- Between 15 and 20 years: Did my little extra jobs allow me to make choices without going into debt?

- During my study period: Did I learn to live within my student budget?

- Did my entry into the labour market with a regular salary, allow me to go ahead and realize my life projects (marriage or married life, family, home, etc..)?

- Did the challenges and difficult times change my attitude towards financial security?

- My habits: Am I an informed and cautious consumer or is my attitude a long standing problem? Can I identify my weaknesses?

A poor rapport with money is like a miserable relationship, it almost always ends badly. It is therefore necessary to pay attention to avoid getting bogged down.

A) Where do I stand with regard to my personal finances today ?

B) Are my assets (assets with a guaranteed value) sufficient to cover my liabilities (deadline to repay my debts) ?

C) If a minor problem happened to me, would I be able to survive on my savings for at least three months ?

D) Do I have a problem getting access to credit (ask for a credit card, buy or rent a car, sign a lease for an apartment, open a bank account, buying a house) taking into account my past ?

E) When faced with the temptation to buy things, what is my behaviour: Am I able to curb my impulses when I do not have the money in hand ?

I really want to make changes in my life in order to regain control of my finances in a medium term.

- Let go of your negative beliefs because the goal of all life is growth with respect for one's values.

- Start managing your cash flow more rigorously establishing which expenditures are priority and which are secondary or incidental.

- Plan a project that will require a specific down payment (buying furniture your next vacation, access to training seminar, enrolment in a course) and enjoy the pleasure of having access without recourse to credit.

- Develop a dialogue with yourself when tempted to make a purchase that exceeds your means: Do I really need this item ? Can I wait to buy it ? Does advertising make me want this item just so I can be like everyone else ?

In Part II of this book, we will learn how to get out of trouble and put some order into our credit record. Now that you know the philosophy of the banks and credit bureaus, we must learn to withdraw from the voracious appetite of the great financial systems.

A new beginning will require greater discipline because if you don't want to repeat the same mistakes, you really have to change your attitude. Through my research I discovered a method called the Babylonian Theory, which is a proven bridge between financial progress and the prosperity that you seek. Very simple and accessible to everyone, this method to manage your assets is not a magic formula based on fantasy. It is not enough to desire change, you must make a plan and take action on a daily basis to create your own wealth.

You are the actor who can go from the role of Victim to that of financially independent. Are you motivated to do so? The cash pump will stop coming to deprive you of your hard earned money... You will lose interest in enriching others, and subsequently get out of this painful debt situation.

You may be doubtful of your ability to change, but if I managed to do it, and then create a service dedicated to helping people get out of debt called Second Chance Credit and then Credit Montreal, it demonstrates that you are not alone in this situation. Thousands of people have taken control of their lives through this transition. Your new beginning starts with reading the next two parts of this book. Because knowledge is power!

Some tools: For access to advice, training or to obtain a budget form with all due respect and without prejudice, go to: **www.bucc.ca** or download a form at **https: //www. budgetsimple.com**

PART II

HOW TO GET OUT
OF THE MESS

CHAPTER 8

THE BABYLONIAN THEORY

W hat you're about to learn may change your financial situation forever. Indeed, we will present a secret strategy for financial success that world leaders have carefully guarded for themselves. This theory is known as the Babylonian theory of risk management. First, here's how the story goes...

Several centuries BC, a flourishing city known for its code of laws, occupied a territory in the Middle East known today, as Iraq. This biblical city was called The Great Babylon.

The risk of managing credit related to relationships between lenders and borrowers was already at the heart of the concerns of the kings of the first civilizations. In Babylon, 3800 years ago, King Hammurabi stated in his Code of Laws in paragraph 48, that in the event of a disastrous harvest, those who were in debt were allowed to pay no interest for a year. In fact, paragraph 48, often mistakenly attributed to the Greek philosopher Thales, who lived 1200 years after Hammurabi, is the first option contract found to have been implemented.

The effects of a poor harvest were transferred from the borrower to the lender, creating a credit risk for the lender. Recent archaeological research has also shown that in the former Babylon, there was a dynamic credit market where borrowers actively sought the best interest rates, as is the case today for the buyer of a commodity.

However, lenders had also, as is the case now, the freedom to impose a premium equivalent to the interest rate differential risk to compensate for the risk of default.

More recently, from the 17th century since modern banking began its evolution, most bank failures are rooted in the inability of borrowers to repay their debts.

For the banking industry, the major risk is credit risk. It is true that over the years, banks have advanced analysis, measurement and management of this risk. It is still based today on the Babylonian theory of the borrowers calculated debt ratio.

At the time of Babylon, in accordance with the code of laws, every citizen had to develop their budget based on income with a very simple calculation. This calculation will be adapted to our present time and whatever your tax rate this method applies to all budgets. If you start from a young age to put it into practice, you will be rich in 60 years, even if you work for minimum wage. You will never know personal financial disaster if you rigorously apply this method.

Here the method of financial wisdom: You must allocate 10 % of your gross income into any savings, then 30 % of your gross income should be spent on your credit debt either: mortgage payment or rent, car payment, payment of credit card, personal loan payment, student loan payment, credit payment, instalment payment agreement with a collection agency or any rotary, and finally 60 % of your gross income must be attributed to services, that is to say: income tax, various taxes, home insurance, car insurance, electricity, groceries, car maintenance, home, personal expenses, personal care, transportation costs, school fees and other service charges ...

The importance of saving: For example: Matthew earns a gross annual salary of $24,000. If Matthew worked for 42 years with the same pay no salary increase: divided into 12 months, this gives a gross monthly salary of $2000. By saving 10% per month, or $200 placed at 4.5%, Matthew has accumulated at the age of 60 years $298 790.58 and above all has gained financial security.

The calculation of debts: by calculating 30% of Matthew's gross income, we will allocate $600 per month for his debts. That is to say: mortgage payment or rent, car credit card payment of personal loan, student loan credit payment by instalments or to any rotary.

Mathematically, if all Matthew's credit payments exceed $600 per month, this means that it should tap into the 10% that he needs to allocate to savings, he will thus inevitably get bogged down in gradual debt, which will lead to a more precarious financial situation.

If you do not have savings or realizable assets, the slightest glitch, job loss, illness or accident, will gradually lead you to bankruptcy. If you add the 30% payment to the debt and 10% dedicated to saving you will reach 40%, the maximum debt ratio that banks agree to grant a loan.

Exceeding this ratio, would mean that you will tap into the 60% in order to pay your debts, thus sacrificing electricity, groceries, taxes, and all the necessities to maintain your personal livelihood.

Enriching the banker: Banks benefit from this situation by providing high credit limits on credit cards to ensure that consumers will spend their 10% savings thus maximizing their profits.

We must understand that in a capitalist system, the primary goal of financial institutions is to make money at the expense of the less informed, and therefore most vulnerable populations. It is our responsibility to implement a method such as the

Babylonian theory to stabilize and protect our own capital and also clean up collective finances. Thus, consumers would be in a better position to negotiate with these institutions and not at their mercy because of membership contracts that favour the lender at the expense of the borrower. Bidirectional relationships give the power to negotiate: unidirectional relationships gradually suffocate any bargaining power.

Here is another example: Marc and Martine are in their mid-thirties they both work as paramedics and each earn $42,000 respectively in gross annual income. They have three children and receive a net allocation from various sources of $2,500 annually. They have recently acquired a property of $250,000 and pay a mortgage of $1,572.77 per month. They have a rental car they change every 4 years, so by adding the family gross income, we have a total income of $86,500.

By saving 10 %, or $8,650 per year with an interest rate of 4.5 %, they will have accumulated after 25 years, the sum of $416 955.87 in savings. Let us assume that in 25 years their home would be fully paid and will have an approximate value of $450,000. Their asset value would rise to $866 695.87, taking into account in this example they will never receive an increase in wages or job loss, for 25 years. It should be understood that if you spend your 10 % credit payment, a huge amount would not be in your pocket but in that of your bank. The expression that says that ignorance is costly applies very well here.

With savings, leverage effect works for you. Here is Marc and Martine's budget table. Imagine every 5 years, Marc and Martine made the acquisition of an apartment building, duplex, triplex, quadruplex ... Now consider the leverage effect: what would their assets be after 25 years? Yes: more than 3 million. And in income now? $311,500 annually, including their salaries as paramedics of $86,500 . Who would have thought that with an annual salary of $ 42,000, someone could become so rich?

Changing the rules of the game: Many sceptics came to see us and we established their planning using the Babylonian

Theory. You can also visit our website at www.bucc.ca in the online University section to establish your own strategies. Nonetheless, proper management is certainly the first step towards restoring your situation. We also believe, that the current funding environment should be reviewed.

It seems imperative to ask our government to pass a law that would require financial institutions to lose any right to appeal and to be held accountable when granting credit to a consumer's debt ratio that exceeds 30 %. Thus the risk would be to the lender in exchange for a premium rate.

Already, our government has proposed a nice savings incentive by offering bank accounts in which the income savings and investment are tax-free (TFSA).

If the majority of consumers opted for a Babylonian budget and moreover poured 10 % into their savings accounts and tax-free investments, our economy and our purchasing power would change radically.

This method is, in my opinion, one of the best remedies to the current financial crisis. And by applying it now, you will see your financial stability grow gradually.

However, the recipe is nothing miraculous if, like many people, you are currently overwhelmed by debt. Lets look at how you can make a gradual exit from this impasse.

CHAPTER 9

WHAT IS A COLLECTION AGENCY ?

In the field of Canadian consumer credit, some people do not repay their debts for various reasons and have to deal with collection agencies. It is important to know the impact of having to negotiate or deal with these agents that are in fact authorized by law to exercise their solutions.

The reasons for non-payment are very diverse: financial difficulties, poor payment habits, overspending, illness or dissatisfaction after purchase by instalments. Whatever the reason behind this difficulty, it is important to maintain a good relationship with the person to whom you owe money and do everything to meet your commitments.

The methods of recovery. There are four types of collectors: there are those who work for financial institutions with which you do business, there are private collection agents, there are those who work for government agencies and finally, there are those who "call" themselves collectors according to their interests. We will see later how to deal with each of them.

If you explain your personal situation to your creditor, showing your good faith, generally the latter will accept any reasonable offer of settlement to avoid incurring additional costs to the courts. The important thing is to tell the truth and explain your situation realistically. Remember that collection agents of financial institutions are trained to detect liars and seasoned manipulators, so do not play the innocent because it would effectively make you lose face and thus make the negotiation more difficult.

By providing a written budget according to the Babylonian theory (payment included in the 30 % allocated for debt) to a collection agency or a financial institution with which you are currently in default of payment, any analyst or judge will give you reason. Because you are entitled to pay according to your abilities and not on the terms which a financial institution or collection agency would try to impose on you.

Send them your Babylonian budget in writing accompanied by a settlement offer, because under good faith and repayment capacity of the debtor, they should not refuse, even if payment is ten dollars per month. In some cases the creditors prove intransigent and they still assign your account to a private collection agency. If this happens, it is clear that they will not initiate action against you because before a judge, if you have shown your good faith by providing a Babylonian budget including a settlement offer, in principle, the court would decide in your favour. You would have the opportunity to repay your debt in good faith.

On the other hand, consumers who do not cooperate with their creditors may see their account turned over to a private collection agency and/or be sued in the absence of dialogue.

Usually, after 120 days, the creditor will: Introduce an action via an Application instituting proceedings and/or transfer your debt to a private collection agency.

Before bringing an action against you in the case of a contract of consumer credit, the creditor must, by law, send you a document called a "Notice of forfeiture of benefit of the term." In simpler words, this document is delivered to you by a bailiff, by registered mail or by regular mail, this simply means that you lose the privilege of paying monthly payments and now you must repay the entire debt in one payment within thirty (30) days of this notice.

To bring an action against you, the creditor must first send you this document which is an obligation imposed by the Consumers Protection Act. If the creditor does not send you this document and he brings an action before the courts, its application may be rejected on procedural grounds. Provided, of course, that you show up in court to invoke this defense. Your absence could incur a default judgment.

If a lien or mortgage was recorded on the furniture or building, it is during the delay period of thirty (30) days (consumer goods) allocated by the forfeiture clause of the term that you would have to surrender the property to the creditor. The delay period would be sixty(60) days in the case of a property.

If it is not a consumer contract, a formal notice is the first step before bringing a complaint to the courts.

If the creditor transfers your debt to a private collection agency, it is an indication that the latter may not have recourse against you.

Prescription of a debt. In Quebec, the Civil Code allocates a period of three (3) years for any action in relation to the recovery of a debt. After that, if the creditor has not exercised his right to claim, the debt is absolved. Whereof, it is subject, under the Civil Code, to termination of the obligation. You are no longer legally liable. But beware if, after the statute of limitations, you make a payment of any kind, you acknowledge the existence of the debt by this gesture, you push back the three (3) year delay.

The private collection agency. A collection agency is an organization authorized to obtain or negotiate payment of money owed to a third party. This can be an individual or a company.

If you reside in Quebec, collection agencies who communicate with you must hold a collection agent license to practice in Quebec.

Collection agencies are subject to the Law on the collection of certain debts that protects consumer interests. They have no legal authority against you unless they have a judgment in hand in favour of the creditor.

Their only means of recovery is to use the phone with ammunition, such as persuasion, guilt and fear. However, by virtue of a judgment previously obtained by a creditor they can decide to send a bailiff to make a sale by judicial authority.

In general, this kind of process is rarely used by financial institutions. It is usually individuals who have been successful in court against someone, that use this method. Usually, following a judgment, the applicants will prefer to mandate a bailiff to enforce the judgment, a question of saving agency and bailiff fees. You can sleep easy knowing that this situation is extremely rare.

The government agency recovery. A government agency is a collection agency responsible for obtaining or negotiating payment of government debts. They are subject in the same way to the Law respecting the collection of certain debts, the same as a private agency. However, they have an advantage that other agencies do not. They can be used to issue a recovery certificate by the court and fulfill the latter by conducting an arbitrary seizure of your assets.

In my humble opinion, this kind of method is improper under our constitution and should be appealed in court. It is best to find a repayment agreement or pay what is claimed before coming to such a procedure: you have still many periods during which you can make objections and assert your rights.

Amounts due to the Government recovery are not reported or displayed on your credit report, unless the collection agency obtained a judgment against you. At that point, the information would be reported in the public records section of your credit report.

Opportunistic collection agencies. Just like others, anyone who wants to act on behalf of another person to claim a debt is subject to the law. In many cases, it is an individual who impersonates a collector or percipient who intimidates or threatens you verbally or physically. In this kind of situation, you have two choices: either you pay your debt to avoid problems or you lodge a complaint against the individuals with the police. These people do not like it when the authorities get involved and do not want to be identified by them. Often, they leave you alone or declare themselves ready to negotiate with you if you threaten to report the incident to the police. In short, the best advice I can give you is to avoid finding yourself in such a situation. Do not hesitate to contact the police, if necessary.

Recovery procedures. If you are notified in writing that your account has been handed over to a collection agency, do not panic. The aim of the agency is not to make life impossible, but simply to recover amounts owed to their client. What you must do in this case ?

- *If possible, pay off your debt and get a receipt with the help of a conditional check(see the process at the end of the text). Once done, you will not have to deal with the collection agency again.*

- *If you can not pay the full amount of your debt, contact the agency to give the reasons which are preventing you. Submit a repayment method as prescribed by the Babylonian Theory. Then confirm the arrangement in writing and attach your letter of payment, which will demonstrate good faith. They are not entitled to refuse any payment whatsoever made in good faith.*

- *Never send cash. Always make your payments so you have a receipt, a canceled or conditional check or a receipt issued by the agency.*

- *Once your account has been officially turned over to a collection agency, it is with the latter that you must make the arrangements for the repayment of your debt. Do not contact your creditor that could only lead to misunderstandings. However, if your account contains errors, it is important to notify the creditor and the collection agency.*

And do not forget to behave as a good citizen:

- *Your attitude in regards to your obligations will greatly affect how the agency interacts with you as well as their willingness to cooperate. When you make payments to an agency, make sure to never give NSF checks and do not miss any payments. However, if your personal circumstances change, contact the agency to inform them of changes, and then follow up on your call with a letter.*

- *Only the creditor can bring an action before the courts. The collection agency has no legal authority to take action against you.*

- *Debts should not be taken lightly. They can lead to lawsuits, which can result in the seizure of money from your wages (garnishment) or seizure of your property after a judgment has been rendered in the interest of the creditor.*

Although regulations differ across Canada, a collection agency is generally not permitted to use the following measures:

1 Attempt to collect a debt without first having sent a written notice to your last known address, informing you that your file has been forwarded to them.

2 Instituting or recommending a lawsuit to collect a debt without having first informed without the prior written consent of the creditor (the company to whom you owe money).

3 Make telephone or personal calls whose nature and frequency constitute a form of harassment against you or your family, or call you on days or hours that are prohibited by law (these hours and days vary from one province or from one territory to another).

4 Transmit to a third person wrongful or misleading information that may be prejudicial to you and your family.

5 Require the payment of a debt without first presenting themselves, without informing you of the person or

company claiming this payment and without specifying the amount owed.

6 Continue to demand payment of a debt to a person who claims not to be the debtor, unless the agency has tried by all means to ensure that this person is indeed the debtor.

7 Defray the debt from your creditor without informing you first.

8 Communicate with your friends, your employer, your relatives or neighbours for information, other than your phone number or address.

In such cases, we recommend that you obtain a device for recording telephone conversations. For the evidence to be more credible in court, ask the caller to identify himself on the phone. It happens regularly that agents use a pseudonym or a false name to identify themselves, which violates the law.

You can bring an action for damages in the courts for the prejudice caused. First submit a complaint with the Consumer Protection Office, and then you can sue for damages or assign your case to a lawyer. Do not hesitate to do so. Agencies acting illegally should be held accountable for abusive behaviour of their employees, providing you can demonstrate this with facts. So, take careful note of each recorded call, as well as the time and date. Know that most collection agencies are still very courteous, only a minority act inappropriately.

You should know that the Recovery Act of certain debts is mainly used to protect the consumer. You are expected to know this. Therefore, we invite you to read the Act in http://www.publicationsduquebec.gouv.qc.ca

Method of remuneration of a collection agency. In general, the collection agencies will keep a percentage of the money collected, which can vary between 25 % and 50 % depending on the date of the claim and the difficulty to recover these amounts.

Under the law, they are not entitled to claim an amount exceeding the amount of the debt for which they have obtained a warrant from the creditor. However, they often inflate the amount claiming that fees and interests are added. Example: your original debt owed to the bank was $1,000. The collection agency contacts you, two years later and claims $2898.38 with the interest. Then the agent offers to, settle for $1500. The agency, in its mandate to recover, may have made an agreement with the creditor to provide either 30 % of the sums collected or a fixed percentage of the original debt, for example 25 % of a thousand dollars. Therefore, make sure to negotiate properly in your interest and politely remind the agent what your rights are.

Conditional agreement checks. Collection agencies can include in your credit file derogatory words about you in addition to the original creditor, and are authorized to, if they are a licenced credit bureau member. Therefore, you will be penalized twice for the same claim. Your original creditor will report the derogatory information with I9 or R9 rating on your credit report, in addition to the collection agency, which will cause enormous prejudice to your credit score.

To ensure that the agency does not enroll or withdraw the information in your credit file, we recommend the use of conditional checks.

Agencies will often tell you that they will correct the information to the credit bureau, in fact, they will simply enter the balance to zero and leave the information recorded for a period of six (6) years after receipt of payment. Which might be labeled as twelve (12) years of bad debt in your credit file.

In your negotiations with the collection agency, you can negotiate higher payments to ensure that the information from the agency is withdrawn or not registered on your credit file.

How to take advantage of conditional checks. This measure will protect your credit and/or to avoid it being tainted.

1 **Write at the top of the check
"CONDITIONAL CHEQUE".**

2 Use a typewriter (or write in block letters) the following at the bottom of the check or bank draft on the line for comments: " The deposit of the amount inscribed on this check is conditional to the complete withdrawal of information on my credit report from Equifax and TransUnion. "

3 Send payment by mail, hand deliver it in person and ask for a receipt, or have a bailiff deliver it.

By cashing the check, the agency is deemed to have accepted the conditions on the check. In case of refusal, the agency will send you a rejection letter, which is very rare. Remember, that agency is a lucrative business and its purpose is not to harm you, but to collect money. Its interest is to make money and therefore cash your check or money order. If the negotiation is done in a climate of mutual good faith, there is no reason for the end results not to be in your favour.

How to negotiate your position. As you may have read at the beginning of this book, the importance of knowing the triangle of psychodrama is crucial in this type of negotiation. If you manage to control your emotions and not slip into the roles of persecuter/Rescuer/Victim, you will not have any bad experience with debt collectors. As soon as you receive notice of a claim of an agency, the first thing to do before contacting them is to know and understand the law respecting the collection of certain debts and get a recording device. Then you can contact them and start negotiating.

Most likely, the agent will try to bring you into the triangle of psychodrama. If you are dealing with an agent who is a Persecutor and insults you, you have three options:

1 File a complaint and prosecute the agency.

2 Send a notice in written communication to the agency under section 34 of the Act respecting the collection of certain debts.

3 Send a registered letter to the agency, to the attention of the president of the agency and ask to

be assigned to a more polite and respectful agent.

4 For any assistance on this matter, do not hesitate to contact our office. We can negotiate with the agency in your place. This of course would be subject to a service fee.

How to avoid recovery gimmicks after bankruptcy. Some institutions use subterfuge to recover certain losses after the bankruptcy of a debtor. After months or sometimes even a year of obtaining their release from their bankruptcy trustee, debtors receive a letter from a lawyer's office asking them to pay a certain sum plus interest, which was already included in their bankruptcy. Paying or reimbursing a creditor in full after a bankruptcy is not a fraud in itself.

The debtor is free to pay whomever he wants in your place. This of course would be subject to a service fee. However, he must know that by making a minimal payment, it resurrects the debt and obligation. Until then, everything is within the rules. The deception is that in the letter that the debtor receives the lawyer refers to section 178 of the Bankruptcy and Insolvency Act (BIA) and requests the debtor repay his client. This of course would be subject to a service fee. The lawyer claims that his client (Bank X and / or Fund X) made dubious transactions which occurred before the date of transfer and therefore, they are non-releasable, under article 178, debt. (e)

Here is what this legislation entails:

178. *(1) An order of discharge does not release the bankrupt from:*

a) Any fine, penalty, restitution order or similar order imposed or made by a court, or any debt arising out of a recognizance or bail bond;

a.1) Any award of damages by a court in civil proceedings

(i) Bodily harm intentionally inflicted, or sexual assault.
(ii) Wrongful death resulting thereof;

b) Any debt or liability for alimony;

c) *Any debt or obligation under a court order regarding parentage or food or under an agreement for maintenance of a spouse, former spouse or former common-law partner or child living apart from the bankrupt;*

d) *Any debt or obligation under a court order regarding parentage or food or under an agreement for maintenance of a spouse, former spouse or former common-law partner or child living apart from the bankrupt;*

e) **Any debt or liability for obtaining property or services by false pretences or false and fraudulent misrepresentation, other than a debt or obligation arising from a claim relating to equity;**

f) *The requirement for the dividend that a creditor would have been entitled to receive on any provable claim not disclosed to the trustee, unless the creditor has been notified or was aware of the bankruptcy and has failed to take reasonable steps to prove his claim;*

g) *Any debt or obligation arising from a loan made or guaranteed under the Federal Act on student loans, the Federal Act on Student Financial Assistance or any provincial law relating to student loans when the bankruptcy occurred before the date on which the bankrupt ceased to be a student, full-time or part-time, under applicable law or within seven years after that date;*

h) *Any debt for interest owed in respect of an amount described in any of paragraphs a) to g).*

A debtor who receives this letter must respond. He calls his bankruptcy trustee who's subsequently washed his hands of the matter and replies that it is best to come to an agreement with the applicant. Law firm tactics are to simply go fishing. The burden of proof falls to the creditor and not the debtor. But the latter ignores it. If the debtor refuses to pay the lawyer for the plaintiff, he receives an unfavourable entry reported to his credit bureau after his release date. Which causes him serious prejudice because with unfavourable information after bankruptcy he will be unable to restore his consumer credit. Even worse, other institutions will only agree to grant him a loan for the sole purpose of paying the applicant.

If the debtor pays the debt, he incriminates himself of fraud. Which violates the Canadian Charter of Rights. In both cases, the debtor is penalized and forced to pay a debt for which he had no judgment and the proof has not been filed in court. The debtor after bankruptcy, can hardly stand up, and often lacks the funds necessary to assert his rights.

This is a grave injustice. Such behaviour should be punished severely and publicly denounced. It is clear that institutions that utilize such practices take advantage of the ignorance and powerlessness of consumers to maximize their profit. The plot behind this strategy is that the plaintiff avoids a lot of costs and attorneys' fees, because he does not use his objection privilege that the law (BIA) granted him at the time of filing of the transfer of property by the debtor. He knows very well that the burden of proof belongs to him and that the trustee will require proof of it to make the non-releasable debt. He prefers to wait and harpoon the debtor when he is helpless after the bankruptcy. It only cost $100 to the applicant to prepare the notice and go fishing for risk to recover 100 % of the debt plus interest. Why go bankrupt then ?

In the automotive field. Another contentious case is that of automobile loans by some institutions specialized in second chance credit. When a consumer buys a new or used car through a merchant or a dealer, he gets a conditional contract by the latter to finance the purchase. The day he finds himself in financial difficulties and wants to give his car back to the bank in the time allowed by law, the latter refuses. In principle, when the consumer returns the goods to the merchant upon receipt of the notice of forfeiture of benefit of the term, between 60 and 90 days late, they settle the obligation and the contract is cancelled by law. Apart from two financial institutions, all the others follow this procedure. Their tactic is to deny by all means taking back the vehicle so as to introduce a motion to institute proceedings before the courts to obtain a default judgment against the debtor and claim the full amount of the obligation without subtracting the amount of property sold at auction.

Once the judgment is in hand, they proceed to the seizure of the vehicle and execute judgment for the balance by seizing the salary and the debtor's assets. It is not illegal per se, but rather immoral and mean, and this is a way to circumvent the Law on the protection of consumers and make windfall profits at the expense of the most financially disadvantaged.

CHAPTER 10

MODIFYING ONE'S CREDIT RECORD

The first step is to get a copy of your consumer credit report from Equifax Canada, a company located at 7171, rue Jean-Talon East, Montreal and/or TransUnion Echo Group whose offices are at 1 Place Laval in Laval. You can either go there in person, order by phone or do it all via the Internet. I highly recommend you proceed through the Internet. Ideally, to have an overall picture, I recommend you pay the required fees and take the version that gives you your consumer credit score.

Knowing that, according to a recent survey, 80 % of credit reports contain errors, carefully check all information contained therein. Some information is not updated by the creditor and can have a significant impact on your credit score and it is mainly those ones that consumers are unaware of. Other personal information such as your previous address and your employers will have little or no effect on your score.

Some security companies offer a regular credit report updating service for a monthly fee. These companies are often affiliated with certain credit card companies. I doubt the effectiveness of such a product, because who knows better than you what information on your profile relates to you.

When you obtain a copy of your credit report by mail or

via the Internet, you will have access to an update form from which you can make changes.

EQUIFAX

CONSUMER CREDIT REPORT UPDATE FORM

EQUIFAX UNIQUE NUMBER: _____ DATE: _____

Upon review of your personal credit report, this form must be completed if you wish to make corrections.

Name:

	Last Name	First Name	Initial	Suffix (Sr., Jr., etc.)

Current Address:

	Street Address	Apt.	City	Province	Postal Code

Previous Address:

	Street Address	Apt.	City	Province	Postal Code

Date of Birth: _____   Social Insurance No. Optional

	Month/Day/Year

Current Employment:

Public Record Information

Courthouse Name or Agency_____ Case Number or Account or Plaintiff_____

Reason for Investigation: □ *Not Mine*   □ *Satisfied*   □ *Dismissed*   □ *Discharged*   □ *Released*

□ Other (Please explain) _____

Courthouse Name or Agency_____ Case Number or Account or Plaintiff_____

Reason for Investigation: □ *Not Mine*   □ *Satisfied*   □ *Dismissed*   □ *Discharged*   □ *Released*

□ Other (Please explain) _____

Credit Account Information

Company Name_____ Account Number _____

Reason for investigation:

□ *Not Mine*   □ *Paid in full*   □ *Account Closed*   □ *Transferred/Refinanced*   □ *Current/Previous Rating Incorrect*

□ Other (Please explain) _____

Company Name_____ Account Number _____

Reason for investigation:

□ *Not Mine*   □ *Paid in full*   □ *Account Closed*   □ *Transferred/Refinanced*   □ *Current/Previous Rating Incorrect*

□ Other (Please explain) _____

Signature: _____ Daytime Phone #: _____

Have you included photocopies of all necessary documents and identification to update your personal Credit Report?
(Ex: receipts, legal documents, 2 pieces of valid identification, including proof of current address)
Equifax will verify the necessary information and mail you a confirmation.

Please check here if you would like a revised copy of your credit report sent to creditors who have recently accessed your file. □
(Please provide a contact name, fax and phone number for each creditor)

Please visit our Consumer Information Center at www.equifax.ca for more information

National Consumer Relations
P.O. Box 190, Station Jean-Talon,
Montreal, Quebec H1S 2Z2
Facsimile: (514) 355-8502
Tel:1-877-323-2598 (514-493-2598)
Email: consumer.relations@equifax.com

There is another credit reporting company in Canada:
Trans Union of Canada
P.O. Box 338 L.C.D.I.
Hamilton, Ontario, L8L 7W2
Tel: 1-800-663-9980
Tel: 1-877-713-3393 (for Quebec)

0403

In the case of personal information such as name, address, telephone number, employer, previous address, previous employer, years of residence at an address, date of birth, social insurance number, you only need to provide evidence and attach a clear photocopy of two pieces of photo ID. You will be able to fax or mail to the appropriate credit bureau. In general, the information is corrected within 30 to 60 days.

Check that your credit accounts are properly reported with a good score. It is mainly these errors that have the most influence on your consumer credit score. Here is a table that clearly explains the types of accounts and their classifications.

Type of credit account (R, O, I, M, C) and method of payment commonly reported (see list of codes CDM for more details).

R	Renewable or rotating credit (credit cards)
O	Open credit account, term 30, 60, 90 days
I	Fixed instalments (personal loan, auto, consolidation)
M	Mortgage
C	Credit line

R	O	I	M	C	Account Type
0	0	0	0	0	Too recent to be listed. Approved but not in use
1	1	1	1	1	Pays (or paid) within 30 days of billing; pays according to the agreement
2	2	2	2	2	Pays (or paid) in more than 30 days but no later than 60 days, or a late payment
3	3	3	3	3	Pays (or paid) in more than 60 days but no later than 90 days, or two payments past due
4	4	4	4	4	Pays (or paid) in more than 90 days but no later than 120 days, or three or more payments late
5	5	5	5	5	The account is in arrears at least 120 days but not yet rated <9>
7	7	7	7	7	Reimburses regularly under a consolidation order or similar arrangement
		8			Repossession
9	9	9	9	9	Bad debt was assessed; Client disappeared

Your accounts should show the credit ratings 1, 7, 8 or 9. Consider the following example: You have a credit card (In R), the number following the letter gives the account status the last time it was reported by the creditor. So R1 means that you pay as agreed within 30 days. R2 means that you are more than 30 days late. However, if today you are no longer late and it dates back three months, R2 rating will have a significant impact on your score if your creditor has not performed regular updates as they are supposed to. If the account is reported R2, R3, R4, R5, the delay time of several past months, and now your account is updated with the creditor but is not reported correctly on your card, your score will be greatly affected.

Here is an example: the client has an RBC Visa card and pulling up their credit file we see this:

MEMBER TRANSACTION	
Com/IDCodeDef Open HC Trms bal Arr Cl 30/60/90 MR DDA	
ROYAL BANK VISA	
*I 08/2007 R3	01/2007 12/2000 1094 850 R3 2/1/0
Cl Previous	R3-08/2007, R2-06/2003, R2-04/2003
Description	Account acquitted Closed at the request of the creditor
TDCT VISA	(800) 983-8472
*I	01/2007, 03/2001, 328 321, R9 0/0/0, 01/2002
Cl Previous	R5-01/2002, R5-12/2001, R5-11/2001
Description	Past into profits and losses

In reality, the client's balance is now $0. He paid for everything, but the current rating demonstrates that there is still a balance. R3 rating affects the calculation of the credit score as if he was currently in arrears. If the customer has paid his account in full on time, the registration number should appear R1. If the customer has not paid in a timely manner and the account has been assigned to a third party for collection, the rating should be R9. Since he paid all he owed, the balance should be zero. In the case of Visa, if the customer has paid for everything, even to a collection agency, the balance should be adjusted to $0. Numerous errors that are found on credit reports are mainly the lack of discipline of financial institutions to report information consistently and correctly. The credit bureaus are in no way to blame in this case. There are many factors that go into calculating the credit score. The enigma is that consumers do not know what variable affects the score.

Here is another example of credit information reported, which can greatly affect your score:

MEMBER TRANSACTION		
Com/IDCode Rpté Open HC Trms bal Arr Cl 30/60/90 MR DDA		
SCOTIA BANK VISA		
* I	01/2009, 12/2001, 3000, 3210, R10/0/0, 01/2009, 650ON111	
Cl Previous		
Description	Active account	
CIBC VISA	(800) 000-000	
* I	01/2009, 03/2004, 1500, 70, 1460, R1 0/0/0 01/2009	
Cl Previous		
Description:	Active account	

If you look closer at the Scotia VISA account, you will notice that the account balance exceeds the credit limit ($3,000). I noticed over time that the consumer could see his rating fall beyond 30 to 75 points, due to his account exceeding the allowable limit. However, if today the actual balance on the card is $500 and the information on the record indicates that the card is maximized, the information is inaccurate and therefore is unfavourable to the consumer.

For CIBC VISA card, the balance displays beyond 60 % utilization of the limit. In my experience, when the count exceeds 60 % utilization, the consumer gets about 15 points subtracted from his record. So for the latter, this can make the difference between being accepted for a mortgage loan or being denied. If both cards are not updated, it will bring down his score drastically. In fact, the portrait of the customer on his credit report does not reflect reality.

We routinely experience this situation with mortgage agents who call us to ask for assistance in this regard. To qualify with a competitive interest rate, their client needs a score of 680. The client with 675, does not qualify, given his Scotia VISA card that is used 100% and his CIBC Visa used more than 60%. The mortgage lender will not consider reading an updated credit card report that the client can provide. It will only be based on the score posted to the credit bureau. "If the machine says it takes 680 its the machine that decides!" They say.

Must we wait for the next Scotia VISA or CIBC update that will take place in 30 or 60 days? In truth, it is the customer who is now penalized because the mortgage lender is not flexible and because the institutions have no obligation to properly report information every month. And finally, the mortgage agent will direct the client to another more flexible lender and the interest rate will be higher.

The client who makes a purchase offer on a property and with only 15 days to provide a mortgage commitment to the seller, finds himself stuck between a rock and a hard place and will have to pay more. Once again the consumer gets the lack of accountability from the financial institution. Generally we recommend that mortgage agents tell their clients to call their financial institution and request an update within 24 hours on the credit file explaining the importance of the situation. Some creditors are willing to make the corrections immediately and others are not cooperative.

Mortgage agents find themselves in these situations every day and often do not know what to do. Yet they receive training by mortgage lenders and this method is not taught to them. So, it is essential to ensure that the information in the credit accounts that appears in your profile is current and accurate.

Unfortunately, it comes back again to the consumer to do the job of the banks, or to update the information properly.

Prior to obtaining a mortgage application, you should order a copy of your credit report to make the necessary corrections. This way, you shouldn't end up stuck where you will not be able to act fast enough.

How to challenge information in your credit file. We are entering the most nebulous part of the credit bureaus. Having nominative information changed is very simple, but to change derogatory information about you is more difficult.

For example, sometimes creditors or banks purchase credit companies as was the case of the HSBC bank that bought HOUSEHOLD finance to become the financial HSBC. When records are transferred, it happens regularly that errors creep into the information and suddenly a derogatory notation appears on your credit file by mistake. I have seen such situations with stores like Great Universal Stores (G.U.S.) for example, which went bankrupt. Another company purchased their accounts.

The same problem also occurs when some credit unions have merged their branches and accounts have completely disappeared.

The problem we see most often is that consumers run up against a wall and suffer serious prejudice. For we must not forget that derogatory account information remains six (6) years at Equifax and seven (7) years at TransUnion. But whom then does one pursue ? Equifax responds that G.U.S. (for example) reported information correctly and TransUnion, for its part, will answer the same. Why this ball game ?

Therefore the consumer wrote to both credit bureaus to dispute the information, but they are both judge and party and respond to the consumer that the information is accurate and it will be on record for six (6) years, as prescribed by law. But how can they confirm the accuracy of the information since GUS went bankrupt and closed ?

Obviously, they will not give information to consumers about how to appeal the decision. Their verdict is meant to be arbitrary and without appeal. Why? The consumer is therefore obligated to turn to a law firm to assert his rights. It may cost him up to $4,000 fee to remove information that turns out to be wrong. Unfortunately, lawyers know little about the operation of credit bureaus and they too come up against a wall. There is virtually no jurisprudence on this matter. The listed causes are most often favourable to banks and credit bureaus because the consumer has been misrepresented. In fact, the world of credit bureaus is a closed environment and they make sure it stays that way.

Possible solutions. The consumer may appeal this decision at a very low cost by contacting the Office of the Information Commissioner. Following the refusal of the credit bureaus to make the necessary corrections, the consumer has thirty (30) days to submit an application for examination of disputes before the Office of the Information Commissioner which is the government body that regulates credit agencies under the Act for the Protection of Personal Information.

I have seen cases where there was no hearing and the case was settled amicably between the Commission and the credit bureaus, in favour of the consumer. Perhaps to avoid the existence of a law which would be detrimental to the credit bureaus and financial institutions. If you win your case, you will not get compensation via the Office of the Information Commissioner. You must submit an application for damages with the appropriate civil courts.

Adding a comment to your file. To justify or qualify the reasons for the delay or non-payment, the consumer may add some messages to the credit record. However you should be aware that this will have no impact on your credit score and unfortunately the majority of creditors will not even consider it. This message will be reported in a section called consumer statement.

If any information about you is not verifiable, in other words that it is true and correct, it will be removed from your credit report. It is in articles 38-42 of the Civil Code relating to credit reporting agencies and it is the Information Access Commission that governs the application.

I recommend you ask for accelerated processing from the Office of the Information Commissioner, or else the delay can be very long. At the Commission hearing, the credit bureaus and the creditor in default must demonstrate that the information about your account is unequivocal and accurate.

You will have to provide explanations or evidence to support your submission to the Commissioner. The latter will require evidence to the accuracy of the file for the instances concerned. Being unable to produce tangible evidence, the Commissioner should make a decision favourable to you, which will order the credit bureaus or creditor to eradicate the false information.

For each of the accounts listed on your credit report, creditors provide a description of the account or comment. Make sure the correct comment is mentioned in the description of your account. Some comments may negatively affect your score.

The table below is provided to members and financial institutions through Equifax

DESCRIPTION

01	SUBJECT STATES MERCHANDIZE FAULTY – VOLUNTARILY RETURNED
02	SUBJECT STATES ACCOUNT WAS / IS PAID BY INSURANCE
03	SUBJECT STATES THESE WERE CHARGES INCURRED BY FORMER SPOUSE
04	OVERDRAFT
05	BUSINESS VENTURE / SUBJECT LIABLE
06	OVERDRAFT PRIVILEGES
07	SUBJECT STATES ACCOUNT DISPUTED – HAS FILED CROSS ACTION

08	AMOUNT IN PAYMENT COLUMN IS ON A WEEKLY BASIS
09	ARREARS WERE DUE TO STRIKE OR UNEMPLOYMENT
10	ARREARS WERE DUE TO MEDICAL EXPENSES OR ILLNESS
11	INCLUDED IN BANKRUPTCY
12	INCLUDED IN O.P.D.
13	VOLUNTARY REPOSSESSION
14	INVOLUNTARY REPOSSESSION
15	AUTO LOAN
16	COMMERCIAL LOAN/ACCOUNT
17	ACCOUNT ASSIGNED TO THIRD PARTY FOR COLLECTION
18	HOME LOAN
19	HOME IMPROVEMENT LOAN
20	CLOSED AT CONSUMER'S REQUEST
21	PERSONAL LOAN
22	CLOSED BY CREDIT GRANTOR
23	SECURED LOAN
24	PERSONAL LINE OF CREDIT
25	MERCHANDISE REDEEMED, ACCOUNT NOW PAID OR UP-TO-DATE
26	AMOUNT IN H/C IS CREDIT LIMIT
27	SUBJECT DISPUTES THIS ACCOUNT
28	TRANSFERRED
29	PAID – CREDIT LINE CLOSED

30 STUDENT LOAN
Narrative Code A0 will superce de Narrative Code 30

31 CONDITIONAL SALES

32 LOAN WAS PAID OUT BY THIRD PARTY

33 COLLECTION PAID DIRECTLY TO CREDITOR

34 SUBJECT STATES- HAS A CO-SIGNER

35 SUBJECT STATES-IS A CO-SIGNER

36 WRITTEN OFF

37 CURRENT STATUS UNKNOWN

38 SUBJECT IS AN ENDORSER

39 SUBJECT HAS AN ENDORSER

40 BALANCE IS NOT AVAILABLE

41 SUED/PAID

42 JUDGMENT ACCOUNT

43 INCLUDED IN VOLUNTARY DEPOSIT

44 BLANKET LOAN UNDER SECTION 178

45 EMPLOYEE ACCOUNT

46 CREDIT COUNSELING

47 GARNISHEE ACCOUNT

48 INTERNAL COLLECTION

49 LOAN/ACCOUNT PENDING

50 NO LOAN EXPERIENCE

51 SKIP ACCOUNT

52	PROMISSORY NOTE
53	RENT ARREARS
54	SERVICES RENDERED
55	GOODS SOLD
56	DUE TO NSF CHEQUES
57	PAYROLL DEDUCTION
58	PREPAID
59	NO FURTHER CREDIT
60	ACCOUNT PAID
61	LEGAL ACTION TAKEN
63	CANADA STUDENT LOAN
65	AUTHORIZED USER
74	ACCOUNT BEING PAID ON REDUCED PAYMENT
76	LEASE ACCOUNT
77	DEMAND LOAN
78	INACTIVE ACCOUNT
79	PAYMENTS ASSUMED BY THIRD PARTY
80	NO ACTIVITY SINCE DATE REPORTED
86	FORFEIT OF DEED IN LIEU OF FORECLOSURE
87	U.S. DOLLAR ACCOUNT
88	SUBJECT NO LONGER ASSOCIATED WITH ACCOUNT
89	UPDATE FREEZE REQUESTED BY CREDIT GRANTOR
90	CREDIT LINE CLOSED

91	NOTE LOAN
92	SETTLEMENT MADE
93	CASH CROP
94	DAIRY FARMING
95	PAID OUT IN FULL BY CO-SIGNER
96	FARM LOAN
97	REGULAR PAYMENTS PRESENTLY BEING MADE
98	NOT INCLUDED IN BANKRUPTCY
99	AMOUNT(S) NOT AVAILABLE
A0	STUDENT LOAN-PAYMENT DEFERRED ** Both codes must be provided
A1	DEFAULTED STUDENT LOAN
A2	DEFAULTED STUDENT LOAN-CLAIM FILED AGAINST GUARANTOR
A3	MORTGAGE
A4	BALANCE PAID BY INSURANCE COMPANY
A5	INSURANCE CLAIM PENDING
A6	INTEREST PAYMENT ONLY
B2	PAID BY INSURANCE
B3	LOAN IN DEFAULT-PAID BY GOVERNMENT GUARANTOR
B4	REFINANCED
B5	SEMI ANNUAL PAYMENTS
B6	MONTHLY PAYMENTS
B7	SEMI-MONTHLY PAYMENTS

B8	BIMONTHLY PAYMENTS
B9	SINGLE PAYMENT LOAN
C0	DEFERRED PAYMENT
C1	BI-WEEKLY PAYMENTS
C5	STUDENT LINE OF CREDIT
C8	WEEKLY PAYMENTS
C9	QUARTERLY PAYMENTS
D0	ANNUAL PAYMENTS
D1	REDEEMED REPOSSESSION
D2	DISPUTE-RESOLUTION PENDING
D3	LEASE - EARLY TERMINATION BY DEFAULT
D4	RSP LOAN
D5	RRSP MORTGAGE LOAN
D6	FORECLOSURE
D7	POWER OF SALE
D8	QUITCLAIM

Period of data retention. When the Act on the Protection of Personal Information was adopted in the 1990's, the government was supposed to establish a timetable for data retention in relation to personal information. The time frame was never established and unfortunately this has left full liberty to financial institutions and credit agencies in the field. It is the community of creditors who determine the retention period for data on credit information.

When you dispute information from credit bureaus, the latter will answer you that they comply with provincial legislation and therefore the information will be kept for a specified period.

However, there is no applicable legislation. There are chances that after the publication of this book, bank lobbyists may hasten to put pressure on the government to put the data retention timetable into effect to the advantage of the banks.

Initially you have given your consent to a bank to report the information to the credit bureau. Following the full payment or prescription of the account, if you withdraw your consent to information disclosure I assure you, with supporting evidence, that most institutions do not respect this fundamental right that belongs to you. They will tell you that removing information would effectively affect the entire system of approval of the financial institutions. The problem is that the institutions are somewhat right, because nobody wants chronic bad payers. The reason for the existence of a credit record is just to know your history. If you remember your basic rights, credit agencies will tell you that this does not apply to them and that they need to honour their contracts with financial institutions.

That is the reality that my experience and expertise have revealed to me. You and I are merchandise to them and the respect of our rights is of no importance to them. What matters to them is to try to keep their system sealed and untouchable.

In an ideal world, a non-governmental organization made up of citizens, which can act as lobby and having no interest linked to banks, should be entrusted with the mandate to regulate and enforce the rights of consumers with regard to consumer credit. In addition, this organization would work together with the Office of the Information Commissioner to decide disputed cases only. This body would be composed primarily of consumers. If credit agencies, public and private institutions have the power to create tribunals, why couldn't consumers do the same ? This is **our** personal information, right ? Maybe a body such as "Consumer Options" could have such status.

Do not forget that we pre-exist these companies and a creature cannot prevail on its creator. Essentially man's creations are to be of service to him and cannot rule on the latter. But nowadays, this idea has been swept under the rug for a long time.

I invite you to read the chapter on withdrawals of consent to learn more about it.

Credit bureaus purging rule. Credit queries are requests made by members such as financial institutions, credit card issuers, traders, public agencies, collection agencies and any other entity or body to whom you have given your consent for the collection and exchange of information.

The status of the application is not listed on the credit report; only the member's name, date and phone number will appear. The information will remain visible for a period of three (3) years and shall be automatically purged from the system at the maturity date. For TransUnion the period of conservation is five (5) years.

If credit applications were made that you did not consent to, you can write to the credit agencies and explain the situation. A brief survey will be made for whether the member has actually obtained your consent before proceeding. Otherwise, the application will be withdrawn.

Querying your credit file. Each credit application, you perform within twelve (12) months, subtracts a number of points on your score. The more you make requests in the near future, the more it will have a significant impact. However, a correction was recently made on this subject by credit agencies. If within fourteen (14) days you make five (5) credit applications from auto dealers, they will count for one. However, applications must be regarding the same financial product. This change was made precisely because consumers looking for a car or a mortgage were greatly affected by numerous credit applications. There is currently a tendency to make shotgun credit requests in automobile dealerships. They use a portal where all institutions can be found and by which the dealer can make several credit applications simultaneously to achieve the fastest approval. Regardless of the number of requests you make, it will affect your score by 10 % or more.

Judgments entered on your credit file. Judgments remain visible for six (6) years from the date of filing. Unfortunately, it is public record and rarely updated. If you have such a judgment on your credit report, I recommend you find out the status of the judgment to determine whether it has been executed, paid or cancelled. Then send a copy to Equifax and TransUnion, along with two pieces of identification and your completed update form.

Criminal judgments, penal and alimony (Quebec only) are not reported in this section. Only judgments related to civil proceedings are reported.

Acts of recovery registered in your credit file. Collection agencies send their files to your credit file for a period of six (6) years after the last payment and five (5) years from the date of cession. Often at the threshold of six (6) years, some agencies send you a notice from a law firm that requires you pay a debt that has been settled for the past three years. If you make a single payment of any kind, you reinstate the debt consequently adding another six (6) years after the last payment. The information is therefore accessible for thirteen (13) years.

Operations listed in your credit file. The operation items are revolving credit accounts "R", instalment "I", open "O", mortgage "M", line of credit "C". This information remains visible on the form for a period of another six (6) years at Equifax and almost twenty (20) years at TransUnion from the last date of account activity. At Equifax, the purge is done automatically by the system without the consumer having to make the request. The most favourable score accounts are the ones classified as "R". The reason is that, compared to a personal loan where you provide an article of preauthorized payment, a revolving account payment is variable depending on the balance used and it requires an effort on the part of the consumer to make a payment before the closing date. "I" statements rank second, they are accounts with fixed monthly payment, instalment loans, personal loans or RRSP investments. Accounts classified as "O" are accounts payable in full every month, such as certain American Express limitless credit cards, Rogers Communications, Telus and Bell Mobility. These accounts have no major impact on the score unless derogatory references are reported. Creditors rarely report accounts classified as "M" for mortgages. They will mainly report these when the consumer has several delays and is on advance notice of exercise. Why mortgages are not reported remains a mystery. Based on certain assumptions, creditors do not assess a mortgage loan as credit. Others think it is because the banks do not want to see insurance companies solicit their customers. Accounts classified as "C" refers to lines of credit and credit lines. However, banks do not report this. They classify these accounts as "R". Again, there are numerous assumptions on why the banks include these accounts in R. Some would say that the impact on the score is more important and it seems to be the most valid reason.

If your accounts "R" and "I" are inactive for a period exceeding three (3) years and you have no credit activity during this period, your credit score will be absent from your record.

Access to public records and your credit. Consumer proposals and arrangements with creditors will appear up to three (3) years from the date of settlement or release. In the case of a voluntary bankruptcy filing, the information will be displayed for six (6) years following the date of release. If the release date is not listed, the information will remain posted for six (6) years from the date of filing. This information may not at any time be removed from the record because it is accessible to the public, as defined in the Access to Information Act. It happens regularly that consumers enter into a consumer proposal and a few months later transform it into a bankruptcy cession. The information in the proposal and bankruptcy can be reported twice as if there were two cases when in fact there is only one. It is essential to provide evidence that the two cases are not one and attach the update form to ensure that the public record is not reported as a double bankruptcy on the credit record. Once the proposal is complete, the voluntary agreement or deposit, the consumer must make an update of his credit report and make sure all creditors who have been the subject of the proposal show the annotation "R7".

Secured Loans and your credit. In Quebec, secured loans are not reported on the credit report. However, it happens regularly that lenders require a quittance or interpret it as a judgment. This occurs primarily for consumers who live in Ontario and take up residence in Quebec. If this happens and you are now resident of Quebec, please contact the credit agencies directly to add a comment on the record or simply remove the information.

Bank items and your credit report. Banking products are almost never reported, if you have had several bad checks or an overdrawn bank account, it is likely that this information is reported in the "Banking Information" on your credit file section. This information is displayed for a period of six (6) years from the last date reported.

Foreclosures, judgments, liens and your credit report. Where a seizure is issued against you, the information will be reported to your credit file for a period of six (6) years from the date of filing. Once it's paid or realized, it is very important to update your record to the correct classification.

In general, criminal or penal judgments are not reported on the consumers credit record. Judgments of administrative and civil order are on the record without specifying the nature of the recourse. In Canadian provinces, except for Quebec, certain types of judgments such as alimony, are however included. Privileges such as guarantees on mortgages, liens or bonds on consumer products (e.g. Car, boat, motorcycle, etc.) are also recorded and reported on consumer credit records, except in Quebec.

CHAPTER 11

DEBT CONSOLIDATION AND INTEREST RATES

Many consumers find themselves in a dead end with their financial institutions when they discover the seriousness of their situation. At this stage, the person in debt becomes aware of the problem and will meet his banker to apply for a consolidation loan. It's important to first know that a debt consolidation loan is a personal loan and foremost the lender's risk is very high, especially if you have no realizable assets (property seizure value) to pledge as collateral. The qualifications for this type of loan are the same as for a personal loan.

1. Your Beacon score must be greater than 660 (banks and credit unions) or 580 (some credit card companies)

2. Your debt ratio must be less than 40 %

3. Your job must be permanent full-time

4. There are no layoffs announced

5. You must have realizable assets

If you are a homeowner and you have capital or realizable assets, your institution can offer you to refinance your property and include the payment of your debts. In this case, the minimum acceptable score can be 620 (minimum score required by insurers such as the Canada Mortgage and Housing Corporation). The total amount of the loan may not exceed 90 % of the value of the property. However, some institutions such as Citi Financial, will provide up to 100 % of the value at a higher interest rate.

If you do not have a property and you rent or live with your parents, the institution may request a co-signer / guarantor with realizable assets. Unfortunately, as soon as you exceed 60 % utilization on your revolving credit accounts, your credit score Beacon drops dramatically and brings you under the standards required to qualify for your consolidation loan.

If this is your situation and you are in a deadlock, first check with your debt ratio using the Babylonian Theory to find out what your percentage of debt is. If you exceed 40 %, you are in a state of actual insolvency. You should consult an insolvency advisor immediately. You can consider doing a consumer proposal or bankruptcy. If you make an offer, you can pay all your creditors into one payment without interest. The impact on your credit will be less than a bankruptcy.

The methods of calculating interest rates. Attracted by easy credit advertising, consumers often forget to watch what rates are offered by banks on credit cards, lines of credit and home equity credit lines. Sometimes, a personal loan from Citi Financial at 33 % interest may be cheaper than a credit card at 19.9 %. Ironic, isn't it? Consumers shop interest rates without knowing that there are several calculation methods.

I invite you to do a little exercise with me. I asked this question a thousand times and the majority of people have told me essentially the same thing, some were just a few dollars off. **Do not cheat and do the following exercise:**

10 000

10 %

12 months

You calculated quickly, you said to yourself: $ 1,200... No, more like $1000. Well, you're right and wrong at the same time. Don't worry, some bank managers told me $1,200. The response is mainly in the method of calculating the interest. There are two common ways used by financial institutions to calculate interest.

There is currently decreasing interest applicable to personal loans, automobiles and mortgage, and there is the compound interest applicable to lines of credit, credit cards, promissory notes and investments.

The correct answer to the question above is $91 549. Surprised? Look at the chart below and you will understand.

DEPRECIATION OF A DECREASING INTEREST LOAN	
Loan amount	10 000,00 $
Monthly installment	879,16 $
Duration	12 months
Total obligation	10 549,91 $
Interest rate	10 %
Interest cost	549,91 $
Payment frequency	Monthly
Amortization period	12

PAYMENT ACTIVITY			
Month	Interest paid	Payments on capital	Remaining balance
1	83,33 $	795,83 $	9 204,17 $
2	76,70 $	802,46 $	8 401,72 $
3	70,01 $	809,14 $	7 592,57 $
4	63,27 $	815,89 $	6776,68 $
5	56,47 $	822,69 $	5 954,00 $
6	49,62 $	829,54 $	5 124,46 $
7	42,70 $	836,46 $	4 288,00 $
8	35,73 $	843,43 $	3 444,58 $
9	28,70 $	850,45 $	2 594,12 $
10	21,62 $	857,54 $	1 736,58 $
11	14,47 $	864,69 $	871,89 $
12	7,27 $	871,89 $	0,00 $

The first month, you pay more interest than capital, the interest is calculated on the outstanding balance each month, it is known as a decreasing interest loan.

Now let's look at the same amount borrowed if the calculation was in **compound interest**: you pay interest on the original amount borrowed until full repayment.

DEPRECIATION OF A COMPOUND INTEREST LOAN	
Loan amount	10 000,00 $
Monthly installment	871,16 $
Duration	12 months
Total obligation	11 200 $
Interest rate	10 %
Interest cost	1200 $
Payment frequency	Monthly
Amortization period	12

So for example, you have $20,000 on a line of credit with the credit union at 6% interest, it is maximized at $20,000. Your minimum payment is 3%, or $600 per month. In 60 months, your balance will always be within a few dollars of, $20,000. Interest on a line of credit is calculated daily from the first day when you took or used the money.

If you change your line of credit into a personal loan decreasing interest to 12%, your monthly payment will be $444.89 for 60 months. You have paid $6,693.34 interest and your balance is $0.

If you add the same amount on your amortized mortgage loan over 20 years at 5.25%, you will have a monthly payment of $134.77 more on your mortgage and the interest cost will rise to $12 344.52.

In the previous three examples the highest interest rate is the one that costs the least. Which solution do you think your bank advisor will propose to you when you apply for funding?

CHAPTER 12

RE-ESTABLISHING YOUR CONSUMER CREDIT

Specifically, when it comes to credit repair, agencies have developed a whole arsenal of deterrent strategies from misinformation cunning, to the use of highly questionable yet legal methods!

How many times have we repeatedly heard that credit repair is impossible, the only way to improve our credit is to wait seven (7) years, and any company that claims to improve our credit score is more or less a scammer? It is surprising that people believe these claims, as they are false. This misinformation is one of the best weapons that many agencies use to discourage people from even wanting to try to challenge the information they hold. It is not surprising that these agencies are so motivated to spread these false beliefs. Might they want to keep a hold on their debtors for a longer period?

Knowing the history and motivations behind these agencies allows us to understand the nature of this system of credit information. When we know the primary motivations of these agencies, we can understand:

1 Why it is so difficult to have access to our credit;

2 Why there are so many pitfalls related to the recovery of credit;

3 Why it is so beneficial for the consumer to use tools that promote the improvement of the credit report and improve their score;

4 How to end the cash pump practice.

The steps that follow bankruptcy. To restore one's credit after a bankruptcy, the first thing to do is order a copy of your credit report to update the information and make any necessary corrections. Make sure that all creditors that you have included in your cession of goods are listed correctly "R9" and the words **"included in bankruptcy"** are indicated for each creditor.

Open a bank account in an institution that you have not included in the bankruptcy. Check with the institution if it is possible to obtain a credit card for a security deposit. Some banks will ask for a deposit equivalent to two times the limit and will crystallize it in a guaranteed investment certificate for a period of 36 months. If you are looking for more flexibility, you can find on the site www.bucc.ca the application form for the secured credit card Horizon Plus People Trust. You will also find all the details and a video presentation. In the case of the Horizon card, the security deposit is equal to the desired credit limit.

To restore your credit, the article that provides the most points type is an R account credit card. This is why we recommend obtaining a card. It is highly suggested to take a limit of $1,500. In principle, if your file is properly updated, you should, after six (6) months, have a score of about 630 to 660, provided you maintain your card below 50% utilization.

Is yours an open institution? The Christ-Roi Caisse Populaire in Châteauguay, Quebec, for example, offers a very competitive credit recovery program and it's accessible to everyone. With the help of a personal loan attached to a guaranteed investment offered by the Caisse, the program should be a good initiative in its community mission pane. To know the conditions, I urge you to contact the Caisse Populaire for further information. This type of loan is considered a major loan, the positive impact on the credit score is significant.

After six (6) months, check with your bank to find out the conditions for obtaining an RRSP loan. In general, this type of loan is very easy to obtain and is reported on your credit report as a loan or personal savings. Do not acquire this type of loan with an insurance company because they do not report loans to credit reporting agencies.

After twelve (12) months, you can apply for the Canadian Tire Option Master Card. This card is easy to get if you do some maintenance on your vehicle from this dealer. This card is a tool for customer retention for Canadian Tire stores, it will be easier to get if you have serviced your car at their store. This card is a relatively inexpensive tool for recovery. Ideally, keep two credit cards for at least 24 months before cancelling the Horizon and getting your deposit back.

A car loan can also help you restore your credit. However, to obtain a reasonable rate of interest, get a credit card at least twelve (12) months prior to the car to get a better rate. Choose a suitable vehicle, if possible below 10,000 dollars. To maintain a high score, avoid credit companies such as Wells Fargo, VFC (Financial Services TD) and Autonum Presto because of their high interest rates and unfavourable terms and conditions. Planning a significant cash down payment and preferably finance your vehicle with a manufacturer. The conditions of approval are often more flexible and advantageous.

Maintain a balanced budget, based on the Babylonian theory and do not apply for credit needlessly. The majority of financial institutions with the exception of the Royal Bank and Scotiabank, will reconsider you after three (3) years of release and three (3) years of restored credit.

Taking control of your credit. To establish your credit score, follow the instructions dictated in the first section 1st chance at credit. Avoid doing business with credit card companies and favour large banks. Allow a period of at least three (3) years of credit activities before assuming your credit is securely positioned.

Re-establishing your credit after two bankruptcies. There was a time when financial institutions were more open vis-à-vis people who have two bankruptcies. However, because of the context of the current financial crisis, it may be very difficult to rebuild one's credit. If it has been more than fourteen (14) years between the first and the second bankruptcy, it is highly likely that your first bankruptcy no longer appears on your credit report. In such cases, it is possible to restore credit. Follow the advice given above concerning the procedure for restoring credit after bankruptcy.

Otherwise, you'll need a **co-signer** to give you a helping hand to start in the field of credit. Start with a credit card then after two to five years take out more RRSP loans, but be sure to accumulate savings. Deal with a Caisse Populaire or National Bank in rural areas. These institutions that have direct contact with customers are often more open to resume a relationship of trust with a person of good faith. Meet an advisor or counsellor, show him your Babylonian budget and show him your desire to save. Thus, if you prove your seriousness, you can gain confidence on the part of that institution and rebuild your credit with the latter.

When you talk to the advisor and you explain to him the reasons why you have declared two bankruptcies, be clear and tell the truth. Do not sit on the "pity pot", stay away from the "it's because" syndrome ("it's because of others ..."). This kind of behaviour arouses contempt, it reveals that you are in the triangle and consciously play the Victim.

The steps for restoring your rating after a proposal. You must first be released from your consumer proposal before starting any process of recovery. Order your credit report and proceed first to update your credit file. Make sure that all creditors included in the proposal are classified as "R7" and that a reference included in the proposal is displayed. Thereafter, follow the recovery method proposed above to restore your credit after bankruptcy. Once the period of three (3) years following your release is due, your credit is fully recovered.

The steps for restoring your rating after major past due's. Restoring credit after numerous late payments is more difficult than restoring credit after a bankruptcy or a proposal. If you are in a financial bind, do not persist, stay away from this situation and consult an insolvency advisor as soon as possible. If your credit report has many late payments, some will tell you that only time will do its work and they are not totally wrong. Numerous late payments on a credit report is regarded as the worst of situations. Because it clearly demonstrates that the consumer is negligent, he did not save or he suffers from a problem with addiction.

There are two types of payers that are generally found in this situation: those in which a major problem (job loss, illness, disaster or other causes beyond their control) occurs and those who are recurring bad payers, compulsive buyers, pathological gamblers, etc...

Recurring bad payers are those who institutions do not want as their clients. When a banker is looking at a credit report and sees that the consumer has never defaulted on the commitments for several years and then all of a sudden, many late payments are displayed during a period following an incident beyond his control, it is easier to recover. If, within three years after the storm, you pay regularly and keep your rotary accounts below 60 % and avoid doing business with credit card companies, you will succeed. Get messages transferred to your credit report to justify the causes for the late payments via the update form. However, if your debt ratio is greater than 30 % or 40 %, you can consult an insolvency advisor as soon as possible.

The steps for restoring your rating with R9. In this case, you have two choices for restoring: either wait for a period of six (6) years to have elapsed or make an agreement and pay your creditors. If the limitation period has elapsed and remaining two years before the information is removed from your record, it may be worth waiting until the end of that period. Otherwise, contact the creditor to make a deal or get a hold of the collection agency to which the account has been assigned to, then pay them following the recomendations you will find in the chapter on recovery. Then get a copy of your file and make all updates that are needed. Once everything is completed, follow the same method explained above, in respect of someone who recovers from bankruptcy. You will provide your application to the company secured credit card by proving that all outstanding accounts are paid.

First chance credit to purchase a vehicle. What institutions mean by this is a type of financing that targets consumers under 25 who have no credit history. The credit report of a consumer who's never asked for credit before, is created when he makes his first application for credit from a financial institution. Most banks will ask for a minimum history as follows:

1 Three years of credit experience minimum
2 Three years of stable employment and residency
3 Minimum score of 620

So how then does one start a credit history? First open a checking account at a financial institution and maintain a significant balance. Not having overdrafts and bounced checks in history. For a first card, ask for a Desjardins Visa or a National Bank Master Card. As we have seen above, a credit card account is rated "R" and this is mainly what promotes a high score. To qualify, you must of course have a stable job and a minimum income of $16,000 gross annual.

Here are the criteria for getting a first chance credit without an endorser:

- Minimum income of $19,000
- Stable employment permanent full time for twelve (12) months
- No self-employment
- Scoring: more than 620
- $1000 to $3,000 initial contribution
- Funded with a manufacturer "captive" (which is funded solely by the manufacturer and not a bank)

- New or Used vehicle
- Maximum payment of $ 350 per month

Second chance credit to buy a vehicle. Second chance credit is a market segment that was created in the late 1990's in response to a new social problem. The recession of the 1990's caused high inflation and caused a significant number of job losses. In front of a growing number of bankruptcies, a new market was created. It was between 1994 and 1996 that the second chance credit emerged at a Ford dealership in Montreal. Given the success of the latter, many other dealers tried to imitate the concept, but could not find the winning recipe.

Through an alliance with Trans-Canada Credit, better known today as Wells Fargo, many consumers were able to obtain a used vehicle and thus restore their credit, but at what price? Interest rates ranged between 19.9 % and 29.9 %, which resulted in a considerable increase in monthly installments for the consumer. Instead of paying $ 275 per month for a $ 10,000 car, the consumer was paying over $ 450 per month for a used car of lesser quality.

The fact that there were really very few dealers trained in this type of transaction, sellers and sales managers did not want to serve this type of clientele. This created a monopoly where only a few representatives or pseudo-specialists in second chance credit grew their enterprises at the expense of vulnerable consumers. Not so long ago between 1994 and 1999, it was the specialist in second chance auto that chose the vehicle for the client. The latter did not really have much choice, because very few dealers offered second chance credit. Dealers took advantage of the vulnerability of their clients to sell their surplus inventory, old stock and lemons from their lot. It was in April 2000 that a new method of second chance credit based on the human factor first appeared in a group of dealers in Repentigny.

This online application system pre-approved an amount for the consumer, so that the latter could acquire a new or used car of their choice. This recipe was obviously a success, with over 400 vehicles delivered in a year. Vice President of Wells Fargo, Mr. Jay Vanhueen even went on-site to see for himself the extent of success.

Since then, the concept has been imported through a web portal called T DEALER TRACK, exclusively for use by dealers with an official banner. This online pre-approval service is now available in the majority of dealerships in Quebec.

This system is available online and it allows to evaluate your credit according to the following four factors:

1 The credit score,

2 The debt ratio of the debtor,

3 Stability of employment and residence of the debtor,

4 The Canadian Black Book value of the vehicle.

So if you answer positively to each criterion, your application will be approved online by the majority of specialized financial institutions.

The target clientele for second chance credit. The client focus is those who have a Beacon score between 550 and 619 . These programs encourage customers released from bankruptcy or consumer proposal. You must not have any derogation after bankruptcy in other words, no late payments, judgment recovery, loss or bankruptcy.

If you are currently behind on one or more accounts of revolving credit, your score can be well below the minimum 550 required which means a very high risk to a lender. The conditions of acceptance will be very difficult in such cases. It should be understood that the second chance is the hope to recover after financial problems and not during major credit issues.

Level of interest rates depending on the BEACON SCORE. The interest rate is determined by the majority of lenders based on the Beacon score: the higher it is, the lower the interest rate will be. For example, a consumer who is released from bankruptcy for one month and who does not have re-established credit, will have a Beacon score of approximately 550. If he had a car loan before the bankruptcy and it has been paid so far, his score would be around 615. So, better rates and better terms.

It is clear that if the consumer has not made a voluntary surrender of a vehicle before the bankruptcy or assignment of property, the interest rate will be better than if he had made a voluntary surrender to a financial institution.

How to choose your vehicle if you are in this situation? Obviously, because you will finance your purchase at a higher interest rate, it is better to buy a lesser priced car at first to restore your consumer credit. Once it is restored, you can easily get a new vehicle of your choice or with promotional interest rates offered by manufacturers of new vehicles.

Choose a vehicle with less depreciation, preferably a vehicle with an excellent reputation and equipped with an automatic transmission and air conditioning. This way you will have a better resale value and you can reduce your financial loss for resale or exchange of your vehicle. Ideally choose a vehicle with less mileage than 80,000 km in order to benefit from the balance of warranty and obtain better financing conditions.

Make sure you have the mileage certification of the former owner and take care of calling the latter to know the vehicle's history. In addition, if you are able to pay the taxes with a down payment, it will help you avoid paying interest on your taxes and reduce your balance due at the end. An important criterion that you should know is that, the lower your interest rate is, the more the dealer is able to increase its profit based on the value of the Canadian Black Book.

What are the best specialized financial institutions? In order to obtain a better Beacon score, it is preferable to deal with a reputable financial institution. If you have a significant cash down payment, the sales manager will be able to get an approval from a regular bank. Banks that receive a large volume of loans from certain dealers are willing to negotiate and grant privileges to those dealers in such cases.

Other institutions, such as Wells Fargo (no longer available in Canada) and VFC (Financial Services TD) are also good institutions. However, since they are not banks, but finance companies this does not promote the increase in the Beacon score: such as a bank would.

IN CONCLUSION...

When you're struggling with major financial problems, the best attitude to take is to develop a realistic picture of your situation and meet with your creditors to maintain a relationship of trust until the restoration of your solvency.

Establishing your budget according to the Babylonian Theory can help you regain control of your situation. It may be that you need help to get through the recovery period.

Several organizations offer tools and support, but this does not exempt you from having to take a different attitude and be more disciplined in regards to your personal management.

Know that at any time you can restore your credit rating, get information and negotiate arrangements if you are in good faith.

1 Prior to any credit application, check your credit report and, if corrections are needed, make them promptly;

2 Defer your application and submit it after you update all your information;

3 Plan your credit repair with savings behaviour and strictly respect your commitments thereafter.

4 Persevere in your strategy, even though large institutions claim that it is impossible to get out of this kind of impasse.

Having counselled and trained thousands of people struggling with financial problems, I can assure you that today's indebted consumers can learn to better manage their assets and most often, they reach financial stability in five (5) years. With the Babylonian Theory, I have several examples of winners

- not with the lottery - but clients who have progressively enriched themselves through determination. For them, as for me, success today is invaluable.

Will you be amongst those who realize their dreams with peace of mind? After learning the rules of the banking system and discovering the dark side of the credit bureaus, the third part of this book is worth its weight in gold. Your prosperity will first and foremost rely on you!

PART III

BECOMING PROSPEROUS, IT'S POSSIBLE

CHAPTER 13

THE SECRET OF THE SCORE

C redit agencies provide financial institutions with different scores to measure the risk of delinquency of a consumer. There are several types of scores available to members of the credit bureaus based on their activities. The score on which the majority of financial institutions rely to assess this risk is called BEACON SCORE. This method refers to the blinking light found on the tail of aircrafts known as flashing Beacon, which serves to indicate the position of an aircraft relative to its trajectory. For the same reasons, the BEACON SCORE gives the lender the position of the consumer in the market along with their path for the next two years. This score is used to determine the risk of delinquency of the consumer.

Other scores such as CRP or 2.0 Consumer risk predicator or the one known as FICO for FAIR ISAAC CORPORATION are also scores of risk assessment. The Beacon score is the one offered by Equifax to its members and it partly reflects the FICO score. Most financial institutions have adopted the Equifax Beacon score as reference. Indeed, according to some sources, it is based on more than 600 factors to determine the risk of delinquency of a consumer. The main factors on which the Beacon score is calculated:

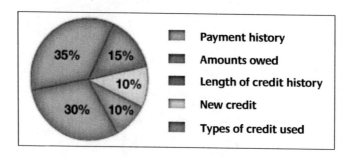

35 % of your score reflects:

- the method of payment on various accounts such as credit cards, personal loans, car loans and mortgages;
- the presence of public records such as bankruptcy, judgment, seizure and recovery;
- the original due date of the balance due (monthly payment of minimum balance instead of full payment);
- balances due to collection agencies;
- the time elapsed since the last payment difficulties;
- the number of accounts paid as agreed, or R1;
- late payments.

30 % of your score reflects:

- the amount owed on accounts classified RIOM and C;
- the proportion of utilization;
- the number of accounts with balances.

10 % of your score reflects:

- the number of new accounts and their proportion according to their ranking R / O / I / M / C;
- the number of credit inquiries in the last 12 months;
- Restored credit or positive balance since the past delinquencies;
- time since the opening of new accounts.

15 % of your score reflects the maturity of your credit history in other words:

- time since the opening of accounts;
- the recorded activity on the account;
- type of account used.

And finally 10 % of your score reflects the type of credit used, in other words:

- the classification of accounts ROIMC;
- creditors with whom you are dealing with.

However, it is important to know the score includes all of these factors and it is impossible to predict the exact outcome of a consumer.

The premise of all this assessment is as follows: Logically, we are expected to pay all cash purchases, if a person requests credit, it is a signal of a shortage of cash or an insatiable desire to consume beyond their means.

The institution lends money on a foundation of trust and the latter is determined by the score that reflects your behaviour, knowing that you are a person of integrity and that you honour your obligations.

Consequently, if you borrow from banks and you reimburse as agreed, it improves your image and, therefore, raises your score. However, when you borrow from credit card companies with high interest rates, it affects your image and therefore lowers your score.

Financial institutions with which you are dealing with virtually represent your affiliations and this provides a good picture of the type of consumer you represent. A good reputation is built on these foundations.

An accepted or rejected credit application? Some people will have you believe that the refusal of an application for credit will appear on your credit report and this could affect your credit.

In fact, this is false. When an institution asks your consumer credit report, only the date, the name of the institution and phone number appear. No mention of acceptance or refusal is listed on a credit report. This is only a report of event.

Institution approval systems make their decisions based on four important factors:

1 The acceptable Beacon score according to the criteria of each institution.

2 Stability of employment and residence.

3 A debt ratio lower than 40 % as taught by the Babylonian Theory.

4 A positive active/passive personal balance sheet.

Knowing the score chart. Knowing Charter pointing. You will find below an old score chart that, even today, is a good source of reference for understanding the game. This internal document gives a good overview of the risk calculation. In the following table, the boxes allow you to orient yourself:

| | EQUIFAX CANADA Tableaux de l'industrie | **Equifax credit risk calculator** | Industry : bank/fiduciary Operation/industry code : BB, FS, FC Request: existing accounts [1] Bad score: 90 days or more late [2] |

Credit range	All accounts (good & bad)		Accounts < 90 days late (good)		Accounts 90 days late or more (bad)		Late payments percentage		Probabilities
	by credit range number	cumulative scoring range percentage	by credit range number	cumulative scoring range percentage	by credit range number	cumulative scoring range percentage	by credit range	cumulative scoring range	Ratio good / bad
961	54,480	38.6%	38.6%	54,180	40.4%	40.4%	300	4.3%	4.3%	0.6%	0.6%	181 / 1
921 – 960	28,959	20.5%	59.2%	28,541	21.3%	61.7%	418	6.0%	10.3%	1.4%	0.9%	68 / 1
881 – 920	16,702	11.8%	71.0%	16,309	12.2%	73.9%	393	5.6%	16.0%	2.4%	1.1%	41 / 1
841 – 880	9,708	6.9%	77.9%	9,325	7.0%	80.8%	383	5.5%	21.5%	3.9%	1.4%	24 / 1
801 – 840	6,392	4.5%	82.4%	6,082	4.5%	85.4%	310	4.5%	25.9%	4.8%	1.6%	20 / 1
761 – 800	4,459	3.2%	85.6%	4,124	3.1%	88.5%	335	4.8%	30.7%	7.5%	1.8%	12 / 1
721 – 760	3,146	2.2%	87.8%	2,845	2.1%	90.6%	301	4.3%	35.0%	9.6%	2.0%	9 / 1
681 – 720	2,523	1.8%	89.6%	2,250	1.7%	92.3%	273	3.9%	39.0%	10.8%	2.1%	8 / 1
641 – 680	1,959	1.4%	91.0%	1,689	1.3%	93.5%	270	3.9%	42.8%	13.8%	2.3%	6 / 1
601 – 640	1,625	1.2%	92.2%	1,386	1.0%	94.6%	239	3.4%	46.3%	14.7%	2.5%	6 / 1
561 – 600	1,453	1.0%	93.2%	1,206	0.9%	95.5%	247	3.5%	49.8%	17.0%	2.6%	5 / 1
521 – 560	1,188	0.8%	94.0%	975	0.7%	96.2%	213	3.1%	52.9%	17.9%	2.8%	5 / 1
481 – 520	967	0.7%	94.7%	761	0.6%	96.8%	206	3.0%	55.8%	21.3%	2.9%	4 / 1
441 – 480	938	0.7%	95.4%	695	0.5%	97.3%	243	3.5%	59.3%	25.9%	3.1%	3 / 1
401 – 440	858	0.6%	96.0%	602	0.4%	97.7%	256	3.7%	63.0%	29.8%	3.2%	2 / 1
400	5,628	4.0%	100.0%	3,050	2.3%	100.0%	2,578	37.0%	100.0%	45.8%	4.9%	1 / 1
Total	140,985	100%		134,020	100%		6,965	100%		4.9%	4.9%	19 / 1

Date of analysis: June 1996
Date of filing: June 1998

[1] Existing accounts represent accounts open at the observation date or before
[2] Bad score indicates a payment late for 90 days or more between the dates of analysis and filing

The score here varies on average between 400 and 961, 300 being the lowest and the highest 961. Someone who has an excellent credit score is usually at 800. This means, according to the score chart, that one client in twenty (1 / 20) will not pay out his debts.

As soon as you have problems your score goes down. Between 601 and 680 the chart indicates that the ratio of bad payers is 1/6 therefore 16 % risk. So you are the minimum acceptable. Between 521 and 600 the risk rates at 1/5 therefore 20 %. Banks act as insurance companies and will not assume a higher than 20 % risk. Anything that is less than a score of 601 is rejected on the spot or is classified as 550-619 non-premium line, usually the indicator of *alternative credit financing or second chance*.

If the score is between 681 and 721, it is either computers or people who make the decision to consent or not, to credit. If the score exceeds 721, the decision to approve or refuse the customer will be made by technical and computer resources. You should know that any credit application is processed first by a computerized system. Then, if the request does not meet the minimum of three criteria, it will be rejected by the system without being routed to a credit analyst. With two of the three criteria, the computer will send it to a credit analyst for evaluation. The computer has no judgment, it is for these reasons that people on social assistance will sometimes receive a credit card with a limit of $ 10,000. The computer is based primarily on the score, then stability (Rule 333) and, finally, the debt ratio. The computer does not distinguish between a social assistance recipient and a state official, an employee or a disability recipient.

For example without asserting that the following are true scores, suppose you want to get a Canadian Tire credit card: you need a minimum score of 635. For a National Bank MasterCard you need 640, RBC Visa 700, Amex 685 Desjardins Visa 645, Citi MasterCard 675, MBNA 675, etc..

So if you make an application for credit and do not have the minimum score required, it will be refused.

Diagnosing your score. If your score is nonexistent it means you've had no credit activities for more than three years. It is therefore necessary to activate your application. Refer to the chapter that explains how to establish or re-establish your credit.

If your score is in the following settings this gives a good idea how long it will take to restore it to an acceptable level.

- **400 - 525** You are now in a financial position at risk. It is certain that several accounts currently display derogations (R3, R4, R5). In a case like this, you should probably think about declaring bankruptcy or consider a proposal. To restore a client in this position, we must consider a period of about 48 to 72 months.

- **525 - 550** You are in a position where there are accounts that have been classified derogation R9, therefore passed to profit and loss, or you have recently been released from a bankruptcy or a proposal. There are probably some updates to be done to your record, it is likely that subsequent derogatory information is affecting your score.

All your past credit has been labeled derogatory. To restore credit like this, it takes a period of 12-18 months.

- **550 - 585** You are a typical recovery case and the work is easy to do for us. It is likely that you are released from a bankruptcy or there are minor exceptions such as R2 or exceeded limits on your credit cards. To restore a credit record like this, one must expect a period of 8 to 12 months.

- **585 - 619** You are in a precarious situation forecasting problems in the short term. One can see recurring late payments or limits on maxed out credit cards. In addition, it's likely to see a recent occurrence of a judgment or collection agency. To restore a credit like this, we must allow 6 to 8 months.

- **619 - 680** Your situation is as follows: late payments reported earlier on cards, too many requests over the past 12 months, credit card limits maxed out , lack of information on revolving accounts. Surely you do business with credit card companies rather than banks. To restore such a credit scenario one must foresee a period of 2 to 6 months.

- **680 adversely,** here is a strategy where you must stay away from credit companies in favour of banks with high privileges. You must keep your credit card accounts at less than 60 % utilization and have a stability of more than three years.

It is expected that in all the above-mentioned cases updates may be required and that there should be a processing time of 30 to 60 days for them to be recorded.

Some questions to help guide you towards stability.

Q : Is it true that a refusal may appear on my credit?

A : No, in fact every application filed within twelve months subtracts from 3 to 5 points per application up to 10 % of your score. Only the name, telephone number and date of the application appear on your credit report.

However, it happens that some creditors communicate among themselves, inquiring on the status of the application and make a unanimous decision.

Q: *Are there secret agreements between financial institutions ?*

A: Yes, if you had unpaid accounts in the past and ask for credit once again, the institutions will require that you pay your creditors, even if the debts are subject to a period of limitation of three (3) years. Legally you are not liable, but you will have to pay anyway. Sometimes it is debt that is over five (5) years and agreeing to pay the negative listing will renew your credit for a period of six (6) years after the last date of activity, the date of payment.

This practice is very common among mortgage lenders.

Q: *Can some institutions enter prejudicial information about me ?*

A: Yes, for example if you had an overdraft, some institutions deliberately enter inaccurate information to make you lose a maximum of points. Information related to bank accounts is reported in a section of the worksheet called banking information. Unfortunately, some banks transform the loss to a loan to subsequently report it as an R rated account for maximum damage. An R account is a revolving credit account, that is to say, a credit card. Other institutions take undue advantage of the opportunity by registering an account included in bankruptcy after the release date. This has the effect of indicating that the customer has been delinquent after the bankruptcy. Fortunately, credit agencies willingly correct the information without charge.

Q: *Why are bank employees kept in the dark about the functioning of the score ?*

A: A few years ago lending decisions were made by analysts, branch or district managers. Unfortunately, influence peddling and information manipulation caused a lot of prejudice to the banks. Computer systems have replaced humans and dictate the guidelines based on financial institution policies. Employees are deliberately kept ignorant of how the score works to prevent them from giving tricks to their clients to help them gain favour at the expense of the bank. Then, if the bank doesn't have an accurate picture of the client's situation, it could make a decision based on erroneous information.

Q: *Why is the algorithm that calculates the Beacon score?*

A: Probably because it would undermine the entire credit approval system. If the consumer were able to master the art of manipulating their score, banks would not get the exact picture of the situation. In the United States you can find a program on the web called Fico Score Simulator where several scenarios are available to calculate simulations. If you are observant enough you will come to understand the factors that affect the score and the number of points won or lost.

Q: *Someone told me he knew a guy who can withdraw certain information from my credit report?*

A: Beware of this kind of proposal that often involves a considerable financial contribution on your part. Credit agencies have very sophisticated security systems; no one can achieve data change therein. And even if a hacker or an employee succeeded, the monthly updates made by financial institutions would relate the information as contained in the file before editing. There is therefore no way to remove information that proves correct on your record. Anyway, ethics expected of the banks must be reciprocal.

Some tips to help you keep a high credit score. To maintain a high score strictly follow the Babylonian Theory, so you do not fall into the trap of debt and overconsumption.

1. *Transact with banking institutions only; avoid credit companies.*

2. *Keep only two credit cards gold or platinum class, Visa or American Express.s.*

3. *Avoid store cards such as HBC, Sears, Future Shop, etc...*

4. *Keep your balances on your cards to less than 60 % utilization, or better yet, pay in full each month.*

5. *Have no late payments for 72 months.*

6. *Do not make more than three credit applications per year.*

7. *Withdraw your consent for advertising or promotional purposes, so the institutions can not check your credit report every time they want to offer you a financial product.*

To conclude, lets review some important concepts:

In Part I you learned how capital is controlled worldwide. It was made clear that the most disadvantaged class generously feeds the cash pump, enriching all higher levels of capital owners. White-collar criminals are often heroes before we detect their strategies. By learning why the current banking system interacts to keep as many credit seeking people as possible, dependent and powerless you have unmasked the persecutor and you can now refuse to play the role of Victim in this system.

In Part II of this book, we learned how to get out of trouble and bring order to our credit. A new beginning calls for greater discipline, because if you do not want to repeat the same mistakes, you truly have to change your attitude.

I discovered through my research, a method called the Babylonian Theory that proves a bridge between my financial progress and the prosperity that I desire to obtain. It is not enough to wish for change, but an individual must make an action plan and follow through on a daily basis to create their own wealth.

In Part III we will slowly but surely become an insightful person in order to never depend on the banking system, or better yet use it as leverage. Your interest will be less about enriching others and more about securing your own future with the dignity of honest persons.

You still doubt your ability to change? If I've managed to do it, if I then created a service dedicated to helping people get out by founding *Second Chance Credit* and *Crédit Montréal*, it means that you're not alone in this situation. Thousands of people have taken control of their lives through this transition. Your new start begins with reading the last part of this book and reread the first if you feel you have not thoroughly understood it. Because knowledge is power!

Some tools: For access to advice, training or to get a budget form, with all due respect and without prejudice, see <u>www. bucc.ca</u> or download a form http://budgetsimple.com/

CHAPTER 14

THE WITHDRAWL OF
UNIDIRECTIONAL CONSENT

This chapter is part of my commitment to become an agent of change in this economic jungle where Victims unfortunately have very little support.

I found that the most vulnerable consumers are under-represented when it comes to demanding respect for their rights. In this sense, the following is not a formal legal opinion, but is an analysis, an important questioning about best practices to evolve. I hope more and more contributors, as well as people trapped in the system participate in the debate and support my position about the automatic consent clause, which to me, seems unfair and out-dated.

I want to help people who have at heart, to regain control of their finances and my remarks should not be interpreted as support for deadbeats. I do not want to encourage certain people to flee their responsibilities or to cause harm to creditors, quite the contrary. However, thousands of people in debt honour their commitments despite the difficult situation: these people of good faith should not be treated on an equal footing or compared with chronic bad payers. Why should criminals be entitled to an unconditional pardon, but not debtors who sometimes fall Victim of uncontrollable situations such as illness, accidents, disasters, etc. ¿

The objective of this chapter is a set of arguments, a plea against the practices of credit bureaus. These private companies are trying to harness a power, which in my opinion, goes beyond their mandate and the consequences affect consumers in their fundamental rights. As I demonstrated in Part I of this book, humans have precedence over the state and legal persons, therefore, one should not under any circumstances accept being deprived of their rights. I remember that, historically, we have created these institutions so that they are of service to us and not to enslave us.

Argument 1: information transmitted without my consent. Allowing intelligence agencies to acquire private authority to collect personal information about individuals, is a significant risk to the future of society by attacking one's right to privacy. At the rate information flows and with current technology, such power cannot be left to state and even less to a private corporation without severe regulation.

Every person has the right to respect for privacy and to safeguard their reputation. Every person has the right to revoke consent whatsoever for medical, financial, philanthropic religious or other reasons.

The creature can not prevail on its creator in law, the human being is above legal entities, legal entities created by the state.

The facts that justify my point of view. Since the introduction of credit bureaus such as Equifax and TransUnion , even today, consumers are encountering a giant wall when it comes to removing or correcting adverse information on their credit report from consumer agencies. The cases of errors, however can be counted by the thousands.

For a wronged consumer, to reach these agencies to enforce their demands is a difficult and practically impossible task. Obtaining a copy of their credit file even online via the Internet is very laborious and at the expense of the applicant, who is often a Victim of the system. Consumers complain of poor customer service and arbitrary intransigence of these companies who proceed to transact with them regardless of client rights. What do we have as a remedy to respond to this unfair and uncompromising situation?

In Chapter 10, I made reference to the French investigative television show "La Facture" in which it was noted that over 80 % of credit reports contain errors. In 90 % of cases, they cause harm to the consumer.

When it comes to correcting information relating to the identification of a person such as name, address, employer, the task is simple though long. You must complete the update form and attach it to your file, send a copy of two identification documents and wait six to eight months before obtaining the corrected information. The bureaucracy here is really slow, given the ease of tracking down and processing computer data.

However, when it comes to removing, purge or change information on the credit information, the operation is practically impossible to achieve. At this point, litigation awaits you, if you want to change something important. During this period, if you have the means to defend yourself, prejudices will continue to complicate your life.

The consumers I interviewed and accompanied received no cooperation from the credit bureaus. They are told that the information is accurate and, therefore, under the policies of the agency, the information will remain on the credit record for six (6) years after the last activity date. **Agencies are judge and jury** and decide arbitrarily whether the information is accurate or not. They leave consumers without appeal and do not inform them of alternative means to which they are entitled to argue their point of view.

The consumer thus finds themself penalized for six (6) years, sometimes even more and has very few known means to exercise their rights and protect their reputation. It should be understood that in the mind of most laymen, credit agencies are government bodies governed by law and regulated for the benefit of the highest bidder, and I named the banks.

The cat and mouse game. The popular belief is that it is the credit agencies taking credit decisions for banks. When consumers are applying for credit and are denied it, it is virtually impossible to know the exact reason for the refusal.

The institution will tell you that it is the credit bureau that issued the decision and when the consumer calls the credit bureau, he is told that it is the bank.

Yet the Personal Information Protection and Electronic Documents Act "P.I.P.E.D.A." requires businesses that collect "personal information" in the course of commercial activities to respect the ten principles contained in the "Model Code" on the protection of personal information, which is Annex 1 of the Act. Credit agencies do not respect this and consumers are denied their rights.

The abuse of the two-headed agencies. To be specific, a credit bureau is nothing other than a private company which is regulated similarly to, for example, a construction company in relation to the Building Code Act. In fact, agencies wear two hats, one as a collection agent and the other as an intelligence agent. They regulate themselves to the detriment of consumers.

It would be highly improper for a construction company to monopolize and dictate to the various agencies that govern construction, how to apply and to establish laws that benefit them. That is what is happening in the world of credit report commerce in relation to personal information about us all.

The credit bureaus do not make decisions on credit. However, they do provide their members, financial institutions, a risk score based on unverified data, obtained most often unbeknownst to the person involved, on which a creditor can move to grant or refuse credit to a consumer. The decision is essentially left to the lender who does not have the ability to validate the ratings it receives. Fragmented processes render yet pernicious errors since they do not provide the consumer with the data concerning them. I call this a unidirectional vision of granting or refusing credit.

The consumer is thus found wronged on all sides. Unable to get a straight answer, to correct the facts, or even know for what reason his application for credit is denied. If he complains, he is quickly isolated. The bank tells him to call the credit agencies to obtain the reasons for refusal (impossible to speak to anyone) and the agency will take months before processing any request for change, if the consumer follows the lengthy procedure imposed. While 80 % of consumers' records contain errors, I wonder why we do not claim a quick change to this situation. The abuse and the injustices thus multiply exponentially.

A personal investigation. One day, I met an Equifax retiree with whom I shared my comments about the gross injustices I witnessed. He answered me: "Sylvain, Équifax... it is a bit like the ways of the Lord, impenetrable!" I told him that it does not give all the rights to a company, because they cannot place themselves above the law and humans. Yet this is what these agencies do.

To correct inaccurate information in relation to an adverse listing on the credit report, the procedure is hierarchical. The consumer must first write to the financial institution and ask to correct the information about them from the agency. The consumer must also send a copy of the application directly to the credit bureau. The institution will send a letter to the client advising that it is required under law to report information and cannot comply (obey) upon their request.

The agency, in turn, will respond to the client that they are relating the information provided by the institutions which are their clients and that under the data retention policies of the agency, the information will remain on record for six (6) years from the last activity date reported. They will toss the ball at each other in this way to discourage consumers and lead them to believe they are legitimized (permitted) under the law to keep the information. But this is wrong. To which law does this pertain, you ask them ? In fact, there is none ! This is a highly questionable administrative policy, according to the information I compiled so far as it proves to be profitable for some financial institutions that benefit by lending you at higher interest rates because your credit is supposedly tainted or at risk. You are the mouse ... Whether it's your fault or not, you'll be caught in the trap and serve the cash pump!

In most cases, the agency will declare that the consumers' request cannot be appealed, this is to discourage you to even think of trying to confront them.

Request for access to information. The consumer may submit a request for examination of a disagreement with the Access to Information Commission (CAI). There should be a period of six (6) to twelve (12) months before your case is heard before a commissioner. The latter considers your case and renders a decision which is enforceable... but more often, it will be appealed by the other party.

Generally, in the courts of the Access to Information Commission, most consumers are unaware of the law and try to assert their rights by measuring up to a pack of experienced lawyers who will advocate for the institutions (credit bureaus). One can only hope that the commissioner has not been appointed to the position under the influence of powerful banking lobbyists.

Moreover, if by chance you have succeeded, you will subsequently have to address the Quebec Court at great cost to obtain a declaratory judgment and exemplary damages. At this point, the defendant may appeal the decision and the time will add up. Six (6) years later, you'll have abandoned everything for lack of time and/or money! Nobody wants to fight and spend ten thousand dollars or more in legal fees for an account recovery of $150 legitimate or not. The legal strategy is thus trapped, as well.

Once again, the consequences will be disastrous for the consumer! It is again the banks and agencies that win against consumers without resources. Multiple experiments demonstrate that banks choose as a strategy, to never acknowledge their mistakes and they will always deny outright any contrary statement.

Ultimately, it is the consumer who remains doubly penalized. Yet the philosophy of our Canadian legal system is to protect the weaker against the stronger. Our founding fathers would have good reason to turn in their grave.

Argument 2 : The permissions granted remain active. Having seen the contempt banks and credit bureaus held towards consumers, I directed my research on the basis of law that allows the sharing of information with a credit bureau. With several years of experience in financing, I lingered to read the contracts and documents that the customer signs when establishing a loan contract.

I knew that only certain information was found on the page of a consumer credit report, in fact, those to which he consented. You should know that the credit record does not belong to the consumer. It is the property of the agency and it must obtain the consent of the consumer via a third party to report information about the latter on this report.

So, for that information to be found on a credit report, you must first consent to it. But how can credit agencies hold information about you without you having agreed in advance and denying your right to access it? There is no contract between you and the credit agencies that allows them to take ownership of the exclusivity of this information.

When you sign a contract with your bank, you allow your institution to exchange and share information about you with third parties. Your bank has a contractual agreement with the credit bureaus for the exchange and sharing of information about you. This is the way that information is found in the databases of these agencies, with or without your consent.

Your consent to share the information has been given to the institution and it will enjoy this privilege ad vital aeternam (eternally). Once the object of the contract completed, the obligation of your debt may be extinguished, paid in full, then the bank will cease to report updates regarding your account, as it did every month since the beginning of your business relationship in a loan contract. But your consent remains active.

Information regarding your account will remain on record

for six (6) years after the last date of account activity, that's to say, the last payment. The information will be automatically purged in the agency's system after six (6) years. The consent to share the information that you signed at the beginning, conditional on the loan, has therefore authorized them to leave the account information to run for a period of six (6) years without the bank having to make any regular updates. The agency's conservation policies have ensured that the information is still present even if the bank no longer updates this information.

What happens to personal information when the bank makes a mistake and reports information that does not reflect the truth? We know that the decision of the bank appears arbitrary and without appeal and that the consumer is faced with an almost insurmountable wall. Even when the decision is brought before the Ombudsman of the institution, the result is usually the same.

Argument 3: Consent granted. Initially knowing the consumer has consented to the information found on his credit report be displayed, I began searching for the legal foundation behind this consent. At that time, at the turn of the year 2000, I worked at a Hyundai dealer as CFO and I was closely interested in the concept of fundamental rights associated with this "consent".

Firstly consent is a fundamental right and a cornerstone of the legal structure of any contract. Without consent, a contract may not take place. There are generally three essential conditions to the structure of a contract, which are the following:

- The free and informed consent,
- Disclosure of terms,
- Valuable consideration.

There are several types of consent, whether verbal, written, tacit or express. As a trivial example, when you go eat at a restaurant you conclude a contract with it. When the waitress hands you the menu, they are in fact the terms. When you place an order, you are exercising your consent. Valuable consideration is that, in exchange for the food, you will pay the money as stipulated by the terms that is the menu. It's simple, right?

When you sign a loan agreement, line of credit or credit card with a bank, you actually give three types of consent.

1 The first consent is one that makes you eligible to enter into a contract under section 1398 of the Civil Code, which reads as follows: Art. 1398. *Consent must be given by a person who, at the time which it manifests, express or tacit, is able to oblige.* It's the consent that makes the loan agreement possible, it is that which creates the obligation.

2 The second consent you give to the bank is linked to the purpose of sharing with its subsidiaries in order to solicit you for advertising or add you to a list of names that will be sold or exchanged with the Canadian Marketing Association.

3 The third consent is one in which you authorize the bank to exchange and share your personal information with third parties such as credit bureaus and credit rating agencies.

Going back to our restaurant story, it's as if the restaurant requests, through your second consent, to use your personal information to send you advertising. And the third consent authorizes the restaurant to sell your consumer profile to other restaurants.

The first consent may not be withdrawn unless the latter was vitiated by error or fraud (deception) and other disabling reasons thereof. This consent has nothing to do with the other two and cannot be cancelled unless one is able to invoke it and prove that the consent was vitiated. For example, you buy a car and the dealer failed to tell you that it was seriously accidented. Had you known, you would not have signed a contract under the same conditions. Therefore consent was vitiated and you are entitled to request from the court that the property be taken back by the dealer and the contract cancelled, or get a reduction in the obligation. That is to say, a substantial discount applicable to your contract. So, unless you suffer from a mental failure or incapacity, which renders you unable to oblige, there may be no withdraw of consent.

The second consent relates to sharing of records for the purpose of advertising and promotion. All institutions will comply with a request for withdrawal of consent under this application. Moreover, we strongly recommend that you withdraw this consent, because every time the bank develops a new product and targets you as a potential customer, it checks your credit report and this procedure makes you lose points. If you have several credit cards and such consents are not removed, you will notice many activities on your credit report. In fact, some institutions, including Citi Financial, exchange your personal information with their subsidiaries abroad. You are constantly targeted by their product offerings and your credit file gets heavier. All the more reason to withdraw your consent.

The third is the consumer consent related to sharing of information with third parties, including collection agencies and credit assessment. This consent is supposed to be given for a period of time determined by the law, but here's the catch: if you have been in default for any reason whatsoever, the consent will remain for an indefinite period of time for them.

In fact within the meaning of the Act, the consent must be given for a reasonable period on completion of the obligation. But once the consent and obligation completed, the second consent is still running without your knowledge.

Argument 4: Consent remains unduly active. In comparison, when you consented to marry your spouse, you also gave three types of consent. The first one acknowledged that you were apt to get into a marriage contract with your spouse, a second in which you agreed to get married before a religious or civil institution, a third that validates the sharing of bodily fluids between spouses commonly known as "sex."

Whenever one of the spouses wishes to exchange these bodily fluids, the consent of both parties is required, even if there is a marriage contract that binds both spouses. Otherwise, one can evoke rape. If one of the parties does not consent, a forced act is punishable in the criminal sense.

Now imagine that you are no longer with that spouse and you live with someone else. This former spouse returns and requires you to have sexual relations with him, saying that in the past you gave your consent and that for this reason, it allows him to continue to have sexual relations with you today. You will surely say no, that you are no longer willing, right? If he persists, it will be considered as assault or even rape.

Having given consent in the past does not mean that the other party has obtained it forever, however agencies and banks are doing so. It is your right to withdraw your consent at any given time.

Argument 5: The gray area of consent. In fact, the consent you currently sign in a financial institution holds a gray area. Because it does not tell you that once given, it cannot be removed, even if you invoke your right.

Other institutions indicate in their "recognition and consent" forms that you are entitled to withdraw your consent, subject to certain restrictions prescribed by law. However, when the consumer actually demands it, sometimes they receive two versions of this request. As a first step, the institution sends a letter to say they agree to the request and will therefore withdraw the name from the list of names for advertising purposes. An underhanded means to outsmart the consumer.

Under several laws that we will analyze together, the consumer is entitled to withdraw his consent in relation to the sharing of information with credit reporting agencies. Thus, it is possible to remove unfavourable information from your credit record under certain conditions.

The credit bureaus will tell you it is impossible to remove information from a consumers credit report. This is completely false. I've done it hundreds of times! At least for a certain period of time. When institutions found an increasing number of letters for withdrawal requests, they probably concerted, because now, in my experience all requests are rejected outright. I must say that when I started to do this, many ill-intentioned people plagiarized this procedure to allow offending debtors to evade their obligations. These little tricksters did not do it for noble and respectful purposes, but to make a profit at the expense of the consumer.

One point should be noted: since the applications are now submitted by lawyers rather than the consumers themselves, the process and procedure has become more expensive and laborious. So far, the result was more favourable to the consumer where the application was treated directly between the latter and the collection service rather than through the legal department. Perhaps both services take advantage of this situation, which seems detrimental.

Argument 6: The legal duration of the consent. There is no law that determines how long information must stay on your credit report. This is an administrative policy supported by the international creditor community.

In 1992 when the *Protection of Personal Information Act* was adopted, the government was supposed to implement a calendar for data retention. Alas, this calendar never emerged, which left the field open to financial institutions. Perhaps powerful lobbyists once again, had an important role to play in this issue... I hope that following the publication of this book, politicians in the National Assembly will move quickly to vote for this calendar. Once again, you will surely witness the weight of bad publicity, which is often the only weapon to change things. We will be able to see if we should question the integrity of our elected or if they act in the best interest of the people, like they all claim to.

Argument 7: The preservation of credit agencies is fierce. Credit rating agencies spread devastating propaganda towards all businesses, persons or organizations that claim to help consumers restore their consumer credit or improve their score.

Moreover, when you receive a copy of your credit report by mail at your home, a document attached to your report warns you against credit clinics and tells you that the agency can correct your record for free. These agencies also take care to remind you that information cannot be removed by anyone other than themselves. Surely I am entitled to believe that some credit clinics have questionable practices and some of them abuse gullible debtors. But agencies have a very explicit message about information withdrawal. They tend to reinforce protectionism of agencies by removing as a whole, any support from outside consultants in a position to confront them.

For just a moment, lets put ourselves in the place of these agencies that guarantee to their customers, in this case the banks, that consumer credit reports contain current and accurate information.

If they allow the rumour to spread that consumers are able to remove unfavourable information in their record, it would surely jeopardize contracts between banks and agencies. That is why they dedicate so much effort to suppress this affair.

This particular case will show us a clearer picture. In a judgment of the Access to Information Commission in which Equifax intervened, here are the texts that were submitted:

[37] I am satisfied that the applicants, Equifax and Trans Union, have demonstrated that they have a likely interest that their response is received. On the other hand, there is no doubt that their success in business could be greatly affected by the outcome of reports. In fact, these companies are agents of personal information within the meaning of Articles 70 and following of the Act respecting privacy:

[38] Equifax and Trans Union are companies who trade in the creation of credit records about others and offer credit reports to third parties about people affected by these issues. The availability of personal information and the possibility of its distribution are therefore critical to the operations of these companies.

Since when does the business of a private enterprise have precedence over the fundamental rights of human beings ?

Other presumed facts that are important to know: Creditors do not necessarily want to ensure that consumers recover their credit. You should know that banks have developed in recent years what is called second chance credit, commonly known in the non-prime or sub-prime loan or B, more profitable for them. Several large banks are affiliates or possess specialized subsidiaries in this type of loan, including Scotiabank/Scotia Dealer Advantage, Td Bank/VFC, Bank of Montreal/Accepta Loan HSBC/HSBC Finance, Citi Bank/Citi Financial among others. So if your credit is affected or has minor issues, banks will refuse to lend you at a reasonable rate, but will propose that you borrow in their subsidiaries at 32% interest.

Knowing too much about the credit bureaus is dangerous. Surprisingly, there are many bank employees, mortgage agents, collection agents who consulted me to learn the operation of the mechanics of credit scores. They all told me that their institution did not teach them anything about the functioning of credit, to insure they are not able to benefit their clients. An Adviser for example, could tell the client: "For the system to approve your loan, you need 660 Beacon, lower your Sears card below 60% of the limit, call Sears to update your file, you will regain 15 points and then in a week you resubmit your application and you will be approved."

The majority of employees are kept in the dark and it is meant to be this way. So much so, that sometimes not knowing what to answer, they will tell you that your application is denied because of a late payment from four (4) years past. In reality it is not the past delay that is the issue, your credit cards are maxed out and it makes you lose 40 points. You are below the minimum score that the system requires.

Today, it is a computer system that makes the decision and the reason is very simple. 25 years ago, credit decisions were made on location, influence peddling and favouritism towards the friends of the directors caused many losses to banks and credit unions. That is why everything was centralized and decisions are now made by a processing center.

Mortgage agents occasionally receive training by credit agencies. You will understand that training certainly aims to create business relationships communication in closed and air-tight vessels with a neutral third person, the potential payer.

Just ask someone who has read this book and who works in a bank, they will confirm it.

What the law says and does not say about consent. In terms of privacy, the following laws (both federal and provincial) apply:

1 *The Civil Code;*
2 *The Law on the protection of personal information in the private sector;*
3 *P.I.P.E.D.A.;*
4 *The Universal Declaration of Human Rights.*

1. *The Civil Code protects personal information*

CHAPTER III OF RESPECT FOR REPUTATION AND PRIVACY

35. Everyone has the right to respect for their reputation and privacy. <u>No prejudice can be brought to the privacy of a person without the latter's consent or without the authority of the law.</u>

This article states that one cannot prejudice you without your consent, so if you withdraw your consent one cannot harm your reputation. The portion that says, "without authority of the law" refers to public records such as judgments, bankruptcies, foreclosures, collateral, liens and mortgages. Since this is public information and is available to all.

Let us see what the other articles say;

1991, c. 64, a. 35; 2002, c. 19, a. 2.

36. May especially be considered as invasions of privacy to a person for the following acts:

1° entering one's household or taking one's belongings;

2° intentionally intercepting or using one's private communications;

3° recording or using one's image or voice while the latter is within private premises;

4° monitoring one's private life by any means whatsoever;

5° using one's name, image, likeness or voice for a purpose other than the legitimate information of the public;

6° using one's correspondence, manuscripts or other personal documents.

37. Any person who establishes a file on another person must have a serious and legitimate interest in doing so. They can only collect information relevant to the stated purpose of the file, <u>and may not, without the consent of the individual or authorization of the law, disclose to third parties</u> or use it for purposes incompatible with those of its constitution; <u>and can not either in the constitution or the use of the file, otherwise invade the privacy of the person or reputation.</u>

1991, c. 64, a. 37.

38. Subject to the other provisions of the Act, any person may, for free, consult and correct a record that another person holds on them either to make a decision in respect of, or to inform a third party, and may also obtain a copy , for a reasonable fee. The information contained in the file must be available in an intelligible transcription.

1991, c. 64, a. 38.

39. One who holds a record of a person cannot refuse access to the information contained therein unless they justify a serious and legitimate interest in doing so or that such information is likely to seriously harm a third party.

1991, c. 64, a. 39.

40. Anyone can have a record that concerns them corrected if it contains inaccurate, incomplete or misleading information, <u>they may also have any information removed that is expired or not justified by the purpose of the file,</u> or submit written comments to add to the file.

Rectification shall be communicated without delay to any person who received the information in the previous six months and, if applicable, the person who provided that information. It is the same with the request for correction, if it is challenged.

1991, c. 64, a. 40.

41. When the law does not provide the conditions and procedures for exercising the right to inspect or correct a record, the court shall make a determination upon request.

Similarly, if there is a difficulty in the exercise of these rights, the court will make a determination upon request.

It is the Access to Information Commission that has jurisdiction for **the purposes of Articles 35 to 42 of the Civil Code**. In Article 37, it is clearly stated that the agency may not infringe on privacy without consent. However, this article becomes void if a claim is in recovery. It is article 18 of the Law on the protection of personal information in the private sector that receives application. We will return to this article later in this chapter.

In Article 40, <u>one can also have any information removed that is expired or not justified by the purpose of the file</u>. The law is clear: if the information is out of date or not justified, it may be deleted if the consent is withdrawn.

Law on the protection of personal information in the private sector, Article 12

12. Use of the information contained in a file is only permitted, once the object of the file is accomplished, under consent of the person concerned, subject to the time prescribed by law or by a retention calendar established by government regulation.

What an accomplished object means is the extinction of the obligation, that is to say, the full payment of the obligation under the contract and/or the period of extinction of debt after three (3) years.

So, once the object of the file is completed, the sharing of information requires the consent of the consumer. Of course, if it is a bad debt, the creditor is entitled to share information with third parties in order to collect a debt. See what was said on this subject in Article 18:

2. The law on the protection of personal information in the private sector. Consent not required.

18. A person who operates an enterprise may, without the consent of the person concerned, disclose personal information contained in a file concerning others:

1° to their attorney;

2° the Director of Criminal and Penal Prosecutions if the information is required for purposes of a prosecution for an offense under an Act applicable in Quebec;

3° to an agency under the law to prevent, detect or suppress crime or violations of laws, which requires the exercise of its functions, if the information is necessary for the prosecution of an offense against a law applicable in Quebec;

4° a person to whom it is necessary to communicate the information under a law applicable in Quebec or application of a collective agreement;

5° to a public body as defined in the Access to documents law, held by public bodies and the Protection of personal information (chapter A-2.1) which, through a representative, collected in the financial year of its functions or the implementation of a program under its management;

6° a person or body having the power to compel the disclosure and that requires them in the exercise of their functions;

7° to a person whom the information must be made available due to an emergency situation that threatens the life, health or safety of the person in danger;

8° a person who is authorized to use the information for purposes of study, research or statistical purposes in accordance with Article 21 or to a person authorized in accordance with Article 21.1;

9° a person who, in accordance with the law may recover debts for others and requires it for the purpose of exercising of their functions;

9.1°to a person if the information is necessary for the purposes of collecting a debt of the company;

10° to a person in accordance with Article 22 if it is a nominative list.

FILE ENTRIES.

A person who operates a business must register any communication made under paragraphs 6 to 10 of the first section. This entry is part of the file.

But what happens to this information if it is subject to termination of the obligation under the expiry period? Legally and lawfully, the debt no longer exists, it is extinct. Why do agencies continue to convey the information that the debt still exists? In fact Article 18 allows them to do so as long as they wish. Even if the information is out of date, because the debt no longer exists. Except in the case of a withdrawal of consent, after some time, the debtor should be entitled to do so if the claim is contested or its motive for withdrawal is justified. However, the institution and the agency may continue to report the information sometimes for more than twenty years even if the debt no longer exists, for the simple purpose of recovering it with interest.

Ten years later, when the consumer submits a credit request and a collection agency appears on his record by reporting an account that is more than ten years old, the new lender will require a release by the collection agency for a debt which no longer exists. But the consumer will still pay even if it is a mistake and that the account does not belong to him. How can he prove that the account does not belong to him, ten years later?

For example, suppose I am the owner of a building and you are my tenant. After your departure, a dispute arises between us and I send you a notice. You disagree because you find my behaviour abusive and you tell me to take a hike. For revenge, I transfer the bill to a collection agency and ask them to enter the information in your credit file. See how easy it is to damage the reputation of a person and undermine his credit?

Credit agencies currently control the climate and make it rain or shine, at the expense of basic consumer rights. There is an urgent need for someone to take action for the greater public interest.

Lets continue to analyze what the laws say about the concept of consent.

19. Anyone who operates a business with the purpose of lending money and who consults credit reports or recommendations regarding the creditworthiness of individuals, prepared by a personal information agent, should inform those persons of their right of access and correction with respect to the files held by the agent and tell them how and where they can find access to these reports or recommendations and to correct them if applicable.

CREDIT REPORT

The person operating such a business must notify the individual who so requests the contents of any credit report or any recommendation which they become aware of in order to make an informed decision on this matter.

1993, c. 17, a. 19.

So as you can see, rather than regulating banks and credit agencies on the retention of personal information, our elected officials have given, perhaps unknowingly, all rights to these private agencies to keep our information ad vitam aeternam. In this law, the private company has more flexibility than government agencies. Interesting, would you agree?

However, the concepts of consent and privacy are fundamental rights. Here are some important facts about the withdrawal of consent:

On the Equifax website, we can find a legal bulletin prepared by the law firm Borden Ladner Gervais dated January 2nd 2001, which states in Article 5:

Obtaining consent! This is the most important principle of part 1. A person must consent to the collection, use and disclosure of personal information about them. This does not mean that we necessarily obtain a formal written and signed consent from the person: the type of consent required depends on the sensitivity of the information and the reasonable expectations of the individual. In some cases, consent may be implied, in some other cases, it may take the form of a "negative selection" (ex: check this box if you do not want us to share your information with other organizations), in other cases, a "yes" may be required implied, oral or written

Once it is given, the consent may be withdrawn.

There are a number of exceptions to the requirements.

Is this then misrepresentation?

3. The P.I.P.E.D.A

Let's see what the federal legislation on privacy and electronic documents say: (This legislation applies to Canadian chartered banks).

4.3.7

Consent can take various forms, for example:

a) one can use an information request form to obtain consent, collect information, and inform the individual of the use which the information will serve. By completing and signing the form, the person consents to the collection of the information and the specified uses;

b) one may provide a check box where the person may indicate by checking the box that their names and addresses not be given to other organizations. If the person does not check the box they are assumed to consent that the information be disclosed to third parties;

c) consent may be given orally when information is collected over the telephone, or

d) consent may be given at the time the product or service is being used.

4.3.8

An individual may withdraw consent at any time, subject to restrictions imposed by law or contract and within a reasonable time frame. The agency should inform the individual of the implications of such withdrawal.

The restriction provided by law refers to the following situations:

In some circumstances, it is possible to collect, use and disclose personal information without the knowledge of the person concerned and without their consent. For example, for reasons of legal, medical or for security reasons, it may be impossible or impractical to obtain the consent of the person concerned. When collecting information for the purposes of law enforcement, detection of fraud or its repression, one could defeat the purpose by seeking the consent of the person concerned.

It may be impossible or inappropriate to seek the consent of a minor, seriously ill or mentally incapacitated person. In addition, organizations that are not directly related to the person concerned are not always able to seek consent. For example, it may be unrealistic for a charity or a direct-marketing firm that wishes to acquire a mailing list from another organization to seek the consent of the persons concerned. One would expect, in such cases, that the organization providing the list to obtain the consent of individuals before disclosing personal information.

For example, informing the consumer of the consequences of such withdrawal is as follows:

In a withdrawal application addressed to the National Bank, the latter accepted the withdrawal and stated that the consequence will be to break the business relationship between the bank and the applicant. So here: by withdrawing your consent, the bank will no longer deal with you.

4. Universal Declaration of Human Rights

Alain-Robert Nadeau in Privacy and Rights says:

This international legislation adopted and proclaimed by the General Assembly of the United Nations, December 10th, 1948 is the central instrument for the protection of the dignity and inalienable rights of individuals. Several provisions are likely to protect certain interests of privacy, but the express mention of the right to privacy is stipulated in Article 12, footnote 1403.

"No one shall be subjected to arbitrary interference with his privacy, family, home or correspondence, nor to attacks upon his honour and reputation. Everyone has the right to the protection of the law against such interference or attacks."

However, withdrawal of consent, where warranted, is a fundamental right which should prevail over private enterprise exchanged contracts. In my view, the failure to comply with a withdrawal of consent is somewhat arbitrary interference with the privacy of a person.

Fundamental rights are above the law and can in no way be repealed in favour of a private company that wants to trade our personal information. This applies to the privacy of every individual.

Assuming a very sensitive position. The withdrawal of consent or revocation is a major issue for agencies and therefore highly sensitive. With the increasing consumer demand to withdraw their consent, the agencies are still, for the moment, turning a deaf ear and they reject outright any request made by a consumer to withdraw consent to the sharing of personal information. Yet, they urge the authorities to take action and make a decision that is favourable to them, so that consumers do not obtain this right, finding themself forever chained in a legally shielded cage.

In a judgment rendered by the access to information commission File **no 05 06 12**, the latter acknowledges the numerous requests made by consumers regarding the withdrawal of consent.

[32] Indeed, as argued by the company and the applicants, the intervention of the Commission is, contrary to the situations covered by this provision, useful since the jurisdiction of the Commission decided on the request for examination of a disagreement is contested by the company and the applicants who wish the Commission to address this question immediately, due to the impact that this type of examination of disputes can have on the course of their activities.

[33] The company and the applicants point out that the Commission has received a multitude of requests for examination of a disagreement raising similar questions with these issues and that this is the second time that the Commission sets a hearing in order to proceed with these cases.

[34] They add that they themselves are faced with a multitude of requests for withdrawal or revocation of consent to the collection or disclosure of personal information and it is important that they get a reply from the Commission on these requests for examination of a disagreement, since the requests in litigation could have a significant impact on their activities and operations.

Faced with evidence of the many cases that the Commission has received, in all cases the latter did not want to rule and washed their hands of it:

[1999] C.A.I. 187.

FOR THESE REASONS, THE COMMISSION:

[48] **AUTHORIZES** the applicants in intervention, Trans Union of Canada inc., Equifax Canada Inc. and Amex Bank of Canada to intervene in cases No. 05 06 12 and 05 07 62;

[49] **DECLARES** that it has no jurisdiction to review the examination of dispute claims submitted by the plaintiffs in these cases;

May 6, 12 Pages: 15 May 7, 62

[50] **DECLARES** these examinations of dispute claims, inadmissible and for this reason DENY them.

According to sources, the Commission received more than a thousand requests for withdrawal of consent in recent years

Remarkably, in all decisions regarding withdrawal of consent provided by the Access to Information Commission, **applicants have never shown up at the hearing**. Credit agencies were on hand, some representatives of the banks, but not the applicants. Why? Each time, the debate has not taken place and the Commission rejected the request for dismissal, claiming that it had no reference to consent.

[45] The company and the interveners argue that the examination of disputes requests by the applicants, do not address a legislative provision concerning "*access*" or "*rectification*" of personal information, nor on the application of the Article 25 of the Act on Privacy concerning the withdrawal of a person from a list of names. These review claims of disagreement pertain only to the cancellation of the consent given by applicants when applying for business credit. However, Article 42 of the Act respecting privacy does not give authority to the Commission to cancel such consent. This is for the courts to rule on, as decided by the Commission in the c Daigneault case. S.S.Q.-life10.

Curiously, I managed to reach some of them by phone (the plaintiffs). They claim never to have been notified of the hearing or some had a mysterious phone call the day before the hearing telling them that everything was settled and to not show up.

Here is an extract from Official Report of Debates of the Commission of the culture to which Equifax participated and raised the urgency to act in their interest about the revocation of consent. The following is a statement made by Mr. Globenski, president of Equifax:

In regards to the withdrawal of consent, when a lender, insurer or other company that provides goods or services to a consumer requests the latter to consent to the disclosure or use of personal information, this requirement is an essential element of the contract, without which

the company would not agree to undertake to provide these goods and services. The lender has particular needs to verify certain information from third parties in the course of the contract, to ensure that the borrower is not found in a situation of debt or bankruptcy.

The position of the Access Commission wishing that consent to the disclosure or use of personal information can be removed without affecting the validity of the main contract raises serious issues for companies and is likely to upset the balance between parties to the contract.

That is why we believe that the legislature cannot wait for the courts to be overwhelmed with litigations concerning the revocability of consent before proceeding. It is urgent that the consumer gives consent under a contract for goods or services know now that this authorization is irrevocable and it is for the time necessary to achieve the purposes for which it was requested.

Our point of view. The point that it is important to note here is that consumers cannot effectively withdraw consent to share information during the contract period. However, once the object is accomplished, the latter shall be in their right to withdraw consent without opposition.

Consent to the disclosure or use of personal information must be manifest, free, clear and be given for specific purposes. This consent is valid only for the time necessary to achieve the purposes for which it was requested.

Moreover you will also find a memorandum written by Equifax on the web and submitted to the Committee on Culture in August 2005 in which the agency gives its recommendations to the government to amend the law to their advantage.

Equifax is generally in agreement with the Proposed Amendments to the Law on access and the Law on the protection of personal information in the private sector, nonetheless, some necessary recommendations are made in order to clarify and facilitate the activities of the personal information agent. These recommendations are as follows:

Within the same memorandum, it reads:

At the federal level, Équifax was a member of the group that drafted, in the early 1990s, the "CSA Voluntary Code". From 1999 to 2001, it was an active member of the working group that participated in the drafting of the Law on the Protection of Personal Information and Electronic Documents Act (P.I.P.E.P.A.). This federal law also contains a revision clause by the legislature for every five years after it came into force. Already, the federal legislator has asked Équifax to act as a member of the revision committee in 2006.

In my humble opinion, it is possible that we are witnessing here a known conflict of interest. How can a private company sit on the editorial board of a law in which it has a significant pecuniary interest, this being the sale, collection and exchange of personal information?

In my view, as a private citizen, it is as if the police of a police station were investigating their colleagues of the same police station regarding a case of police brutality. Or ironically, as if bikers advised the Minister of Public Safety on the committee drafting the Law on money laundering and proceeds of crime. It would make no sense, right? Yet when it comes to police brutality or serious crime, the investigation is assigned to a police station in another jurisdiction for the investigation to be impartial.

Later in this same memorandum we read this:

For its part, Quebec was the first province to adopt such a legislation, Equifax has been working in collaboration with the government for a long time. At first during the drafting and now in the revision of the Access Act and on the "protection of personal information in the private sector" Act. In February 1993, Equifax submitted a detailed memoire to the Commission about Bill 68: Act on the protection of personal information in the private sector. It also actively participated in the debate surrounding the adoption of this law.

Subsequently Equifax organized numerous conferences and presentations in Montreal, Quebec and Toronto to inform its customers of their obligations under this law.

Does this not seem strange to you ?

In September 1997, Équifax appointed itself the duty of submitting its analysis and comments on the five-year report of the Committee of Access to Information on the implementation of the law on access as well as the Law on the protection of personnel information in the private sector to participate in the general consultation by the Committee on Culture of the national assembly on the Bill. 451 Law amending the Law on access to documents held by public bodies and the protection of personal information, the law on the protection of personal information in the private sector and other legislative provisions in 1998.

Equifax still believes that the five-year revision of the Law on the protection of personal information in the private sector is a privileged opportunity to maintain the communication and cooperation with the Assembly.

As you can see, Equifax's powerful lobbyists intervened to serve their cause. In this case, do you believe that as a consumer, you would "be impartial" before the commission ? When discovering later in this paper, that Equifax makes recommendations regarding Article 12 of the Law on the protection of personal information in the private sector in relation to the conservation schedule which is still not active:

The application of Article 12 of the law on *the Protection of personal information in the private sector* has been a jurisprudential debate in the C. Fugère case involving Equifax Canada Inc. In this, the courts have confirmed that only the government had the authority to establish a retention calendar for of personal information and that the Access to Information Commission, in the absence of such a retention calendar, could not rule on the out-dated nature of an information contained in a consumers credit file. It is important that certain information remains on a consumer's credit file for a certain period of time (depending on the nature of the information contained in the credit file it is usually a period of six years.) For this reason, **we recommend no change is made to sections 12 and 90 of the law on the Protection of personal information in the private sector and, on the contrary, that the government hastens to seek the** advice of the Access to Information Commission relating to a retention calendar so that it is established with respect to the information contained in a consumer's credit file.

The problem here is one possible loophole or a gray area, leaving the field completely free for agencies to decide the period of retention of personal information as well as to have their own way of applying the law on withdrawal of consent. They do not respect the basic rights of consumers who request a withdrawal of consent.

Although they urged the government to establish a time-table for the retention of data for the purpose of preventing a consumer to withdraw consent to the sharing of information, it is nevertheless that the withdrawal of consent is a right. Whether there is a schedule or not, the consumer is entitled, once the object of the record is accomplished, to withdraw their consent if they so wish to.

An approach based on community consent. In my view, the agency somehow makes reference to the concept of community consent. This means that the majority accepts this practice. With regard to fundamental rights, there are two types of consent: individual consent and community consent. Read the following in this regard:

The credit record: a practice known and accepted. In this day and age, consumers who wish to borrow money or buy goods on credit know, once the lender has obtained their consent, the latter will access and analyze their credit history. This authorized and legitimate analysis of credit records by financial institutions and other lenders is now part of entrepreneurial procedures. This widespread practice is known and accepted by consumers. In fact, communication through Equifax of the information contained on a consumer credit report to a potential lender will accelerate the credit obtainment process.

The consumer therefore also derives a significant and concrete benefit from the activities of personal information agents.

Individual consent. Vie privée et droits fondamentaux[23], we read:

Individual consent is that which is given expressly or, in some cases, implied by an individual and often results in the waiver of a constitutional right. Individual consent will generally be sought by state officials to expedite an investigation, but it also must be admitted to obviate the application of constitutional guarantees.

And later in this chapter:

Relying on several decisions of American courts below, Professor La Fave asserts that the consent may be withdrawn at any time and items seized pursuant to it must be returned to the individual.

2. COMMUNITY INDIVIDUAL CONSENT

In our political system, community consent essentially translates by the ascertainment of the existence of a rule of law or by the recognition of a rule of "common law" by the courts.

The fact that the majority consent by their silence, in my opinion, gives them the right to establish their policy as a rule of law. The fact that we passively consent, somehow we give up our constitutional rights. Did you know that?

Consent relating to the recovery of a debt. In several postal exchanges with agencies and banks, reference to section 18.1 of *the Law on protection of personal information in the private sector*, has come up several times and is an important point of debate. Within the meaning of the law, it is appropriate that a creditor be able to assign a bad debt to a third party for collection without the consent of the debtor. But once the debt is paid in full, is the purpose of the record not fulfilled? Why then would the creditors and collection agencies continue to share information about this account if the consent is withdrawn? If the debt is paid, then why continue, to punish you? Ah yes, I forgot, because they probably want to lend you at a higher interest rate!

---

23   Voir A.-Robert Nadeau, Vie privée et droits fondamentaux.

1. Consent not required.

A person operating an enterprise may, without the consent of the person concerned, disclose personal information contained in a file he holds on others:

9° a person who, under the law, may recover debts on behalf of others and who requires it for that purpose in the exercise of their functions;

9.1° to a person if the information is necessary for the purposes of collecting a debt of the company;

COMMUNICATION WITH ARCHIVE SERVICES.
Access and correction of a record

19. *Anyone who operates a business with the purpose of lending money and becomes aware of credit reports or recommendations regarding the creditworthiness of individuals, prepared by a personal information agent, must inform such persons of their right to access and correct the file held by the agent and tell them how and where they can have access to these reports or recommendations and have them corrected if necessary.*

Credit Report

The person operating such a business must notify the physical person who so requests the contents of any credit report or any recommendations which it is aware of, in order to make decisions, which concern that person.

If the consumer has paid 100 % of his debt, I do not see why it would not be right to request withdrawal of consent after full payment or if the debt is subject to a period of limitation.

Leaving derogatory information on a consumer's credit record provides certain advantages to banks. I believe you understand this now.

Let's see how our information is treated in public institutions, and how the notion of consent is important. You will discover that each organization has set up its own data retention calendar.

Here are a few paragraphs from the **"GUIDE FOR THE PROTECTION OF PERSONAL INFORMATION IN THE DEVELOPMENT OF INFORMATION SYSTEMS"**

6. To require consent for communication between public organizations

Articles 53 and 59 **Personal information remains inaccessible until the person concerned has consented to its disclosure.** *Consequently only those organizations that the person concerned has allowed may access their personal information. The consent relates strictly to the disclosure of personal information and should be formulated manifest, free, clear, specific, limited in time and may be terminated at any time. The right to privacy implies that a person has some control over the flow of information concerning them. You must therefore ensure that personal information cannot circulate without permission of the person concerned, including the assessment of the means by which you obtain this consent, the limits that you assign to it and the use you make of it.*

SPECIFICALLY

6.1 You can demonstrate that consent to the communication of the persons concerned:

Manifest – *evidenced by a document (technological or paper;*
Free – *expressed unconditionally without constraints, threats or promises;*
Clear – *made with an awareness of its scope;*
Specific – *authorizing the disclosure of personal information given, to given persons , for given means, at a given time;*
Limited in time – *valid for the required time for the completion of the means for which it is requested.*

*10. **Limit the duration of retention of personal information***

Articles 73 et 102.1 **You are required to irreversibly destroy any personal information when the purpose for which it was collected has been accomplished.** *This obligation, which aims to* *reduce the likelihood that personal information be used for purposes other than those for which they were intended, is accompanied by an important caveat: the Archives Act and, more specifically, the organizations conservation schedule.*

An agency may not retain personal information it holds beyond the limits prescribed by the retention calendar, regardless of the medium used. Your retention deadlines must take account of access requests that would invoke the person concerned as a result of decisions made about him but still be restricted to a time interval required for the personal information so it can play the role for which it is intended.

You may have noticed in reading these paragraphs or even better that the guidebook itself, departments and agencies are very respectful of the nature of the information they receive and the desire to protect the privacy of individuals. One must see the nuance between an organization, which has as its purpose the collection of information in order to properly serve its clients and a credit reporting agency that sells information to its members for profit. It is clear that the latter is stingy with any information that could bring him gains. This is why these agencies exert so much pressure on elected officials and participate in all kinds of dialogue initiatives concerning personal information.

For example, just think of the Victims of the flood in spring 2011 in Montérégie. These people are Victims of circumstances beyond their control. Yet the government has taken steps to compensate Victims whose property was flooded. But what about their financial situation? Regarding their consumer credit, there is no measure or exception allowing them to justify delays in payment or loss of residential property. Their credit record will likely be affected or completely destroyed for the next six years. Are these consumers not entitled to request a withdrawal of consent, once their accounts are acquitted?

REASONS FOR WHICH A CONSUMER IS ENTITLED TO REMOVE HIS CONSENT TO THE INFORMATION SHARING WITH AGENCIES.

CASE NO 1 The consumer was solicited at the entrance of a store and was offered the store's credit card. The clerk told him to take advantage of a 10 % discount on the purchase of goods, but he must adhere to the store credit card. The clerk completes the application then asks him to sign. To take advantage of the discount, the consumer thus applied for the credit card. He received the card in the mail a few weeks later. After reading the terms and conditions of the membership application, he decided to cancel the offer and returned the card to the issuer.

A few months later, looking at his credit report, he realizes that his credit score has dropped several points. He sees on his sheet the credit card application which appears with the reference "closed at consumer's request." However, the card issuer was not a bank but a finance company. The type of lender you are dealing with has an impact on the calculation of the score credit rating and therefore affects the odds of the latter. In this case, the object having been accomplished, the consumer is entitled to withdraw consent.

CASE NO 2 A person buys a cell phone in a shop. The telephone company conducts a credit check and grants the phone and the service contract to the client. A few weeks later, the person receives the invoice and notices that his phone has been "cloned". He notifies his phone provider and the latter informs him that this is impossible. A few months later, the bill amounts to over $ 4000. The client files a complaint with the police, but they do not have the budget nor resources to conduct such an investigation.

The service provider proceeds to investigate and acts as both judge and interested party by saying that the "cloning" of the SIM card is impossible. While the evidence is conclusive on the invoices, the supplier decides arbitrarily that the client is wrong. Then, the recovery process begins and the account is reported with a major default on the credit file of the client. The phone provider sells the account to several collection agencies that, in turn, show a waiver on the credit reports of the client.

Unable to benefit from a speedy and favourable investigation, the innocent client is left with a serious prejudice that will follow for ten (10) years. He would be entitled to request a withdrawal of consent.

CASE NO 3 a customer moves and returns the device to the satellite video store near his home. The clerk who receives the device fails to register that the device is returned and a year later, the customer receives a call from a collection agent. The client specifies that the device has been returned, but the agent will not listen and requires a payment of $300. The client refuses and hangs up the phone. A few weeks later he meets with his banker to renew his mortgage and learns that the collection agency appears on his record. His banker informs he cannot renew his mortgage on the same terms, unless he obtains a discharge from the agency, and the mortgage interest rate just went from 3.99 % to 7.5 %.

The client returns to his former satellite video store to discover that the store has moved and the clerk left the company a long ago. As he is now a week from his mortgage renewal, he cannot undertake steps to enforce his rights. He decides to pay the agency and get a receipt. However, the information will remain on file for six (6) years from the date of payment. In this case, the customer is entitled to withdraw consent to the agency, because the object is completed and paid.

CASE NO 4 A customer fails to pay a credit card and it displays R9 on his credit record with a balance due of $386. The account is sold to several collection agencies and the same debt appears three times on the customer's credit record. The creditor failed to exercise his right of appeal and chose to register it in the profit and loss account.

Five years pass and the customer wishes to purchase a property with his spouse who has excellent credit. At the time of approval, the lender requires that the debt be paid even if it is subject to prescription. When the client contacts the collection agency to settle, they make a credit inquiry, they see the mortgage application on the customer's credit sheet and learn that the condition of approval of the lender's payment is the payment of debt due to the agency.

The agent seeing the consumer at his mercy tells him that the total debt with interest now stands at $2,346.67. The consumer has no other choice, he will pay his debt and it will appear again for a period of six (6) years.

So the customer has been penalized eleven (11) years and has paid six times the amount due to an agency for a debt that was the subject of a prescription. The customer is entitled to request a withdrawal of individual consent from the three agencies which appear on his record and with the main creditor.

CASE NO 5 A consumer suffers an accident at work and as he only receives 60% of his salary, he is struggling to make ends meet. Hospitalized for several months and needing special care, it is his wife who makes the minimum payments on their credit cards. After a few months the situation has improved. Then arbitrarily, the CSST requires an evaluation by a physician that they appoint. The latter gives a diagnosis indicating that the client is able to return to work, and therefore the CSST stops paying benefits.

Two other doctors are of different opinion and file for a review of the client file. The consumer finds himself several months without income and unable to pay these accounts. Yet, for more than twenty years, he paid like clockwork. Now, because of a situation he cannot control and in which he is a victim, his credit is affected. A few months later, he wins his case in court and reimburses all his debts. But alas, his credit is destroyed for six (6) years. Having paid all his creditors and not being responsible for the accident, the client should be able to withdraw consent to certain creditors.

CASE NO 6 A customer has filed an assignment in bankruptcy in 2009 and was released in 2010. A year later, he receives a letter from a lawyer by mail giving notice to repay the sum of $8,344 to the X bank under section 178 of the Bankruptcy and Insolvency Act. Some creditors use this unscrupulous tactic in an attempt to steal money from the customer through deception. The intention of the creditor is simply to go fishing.

Here's what the letter refers to:

178. An order of discharge does not release the bankrupt[24]

d) Any debt or liability arising out of fraud, embezzlement, misappropriation or defalcation while acting in the province of Quebec, as a trustee or administrator of the property of others or, in other provinces, as trustee;

e) <u>Any debt or liability for obtaining property by false pretences or false and fraudulent presentation of the facts;</u>

The client who receives this letter finds himself constrained with two possibilities: either to pay the amount demanded, or see his credit tainted. And what's worse after a bankruptcy than a negative entry on a credit report.

In fact, the burden of proof shifts to the creditors and it is up to them to prove that there has been misrepresentation or fraud and ask a court to decide the issue. But the creditors strategy behind this behaviour is very simple. Rather than express his right to object in the bankruptcy process, he waits silently, like a shark who turns around and catches its Victim once it is no longer under the protection of the bankruptcy Act.

If the creditor is not able to prove what he accuses the client of, the client is entitled to withdraw consent.

CASE NO 7 A customer is dealing with a furniture store and finances the purchase through a finance company. A few weeks later, the merchant went bankrupt and the customer does not receive all the goods he had bought. He continued his payments with the company and honoured his obligation. A few months pass and the finance company takes over the payments in the customer's account. It communicates with him and he learns that the finance company was bought by another and that his

---

24 Voir A.-Robert Nadeau, Vie privée et droits fondamentaux, Éditions Carswell p. 314-316

account was transferred to the new company. An employee tells him he is currently three months behind on his loan. He settles immediately and updates himself. A few months later he discovers, to his amazement that his account with the first finance company is displayed at R3, two (2) late payments. The account with the new company appears and registers at R1, paid and current as agreed.

The client requests a correction to his credit report from the agency. He was told that after investigating the issue, the information is accurate and will remain on his credit record for six (6) years.

In such an impasse, the client addresses the Access to information Commission and registers a request for examination of a disagreement. Since the merchant has declared bankruptcy and because the second one acquired the finance company, the customer is entitled to revoke its consent to the first company and to cancel the registration, but could not withdraw his consent to the second company, because the object of the contract is not yet completed.

WHAT SHOULD THE CONDITIONS TO WITHDRAW OF CONSENT RELATED TO INFORMATION SHARING BE ?

For consent to be removed, the basis of the law is simple and, in my opinion, should be based simply on the realization of the object.

This type of manoeuvre is not intended for all consumers, I don't believe that tomorrow morning thousands of consumers will withdraw their consent unreasonably. Moreover, it's to a consumer's benefit that information relating to the credit remain on file for a certain period of time to reflect their payment habits and general behaviour towards future lenders. The withdrawal of consent shall only apply in certain actions and in a specific context. Among other things, the client is a Victim of circumstances beyond his control, such as ecological disaster, earthquake, accident, plane crash, fatal disease, arbitrary decision of an administrative tribunal such as CSST, SAAQ or the VCI. (These organizations rely on the principle of private insurance, which means that the repetitive challenge depletes the beneficiary and therefore makes them save money).

The withdrawal request is not automatic, it must first be invoked by the consumer and must be heard by an independent and specialized court in the field that will make a fair and just decision. You'll find my suggestions about this tribunal in the recommendations section further in the next chapter.

Credit agencies and institutions should comply with the decision, in the same manner as a judgment and the decision would thus be binding. However, I repeat once more, the condition of repayment would be paramount. For a withdrawal to be authorized, the account must be paid.

In the case where the consumer is Victim to an Act of God or an arbitrary decision of an organization as mentioned above, the lawyer appointed to render a decision in favour of withdrawal would require the institution to remove the information from the credit report of the debtor or reduce it to a "1" rating, once everything has been refunded. In the meantime, the institution would be required to establish a payment plan for the debtor according to his budget.

In general we found the best results were when the consumer was dealing with the collections department of financial institutions rather than the legal service. In many cases, if the client has paid for everything, they will agree to withdraw the information, even if it goes against the policy of the bank.

In short, I do not see why a debtor who, despite some difficulties or situation beyond his control, honouring his commitments in full, would be treated the same way as one negligent towards his creditors.

I believe that as informed consumers, we should do something to change this practice. Your support can be registered on the website www.bucc.ca

Why? Because the doors of economic recovery remain

closed to any change in status when our rating remains tainted and in perpetuity. As I wish to assist you in prosperity, I invite you to take it a step further.

CHAPTER 15

THE BABYLONIAN THEORY IN ACTION

My exposé ends here with a sense of accomplishment. I convey this to you, in all modesty, because I'm not an expert, but an informed citizen with a passion for social justice. Admittedly, I'm not a historian, economist, lawyer or psychologist, but I wanted to bring this information regarding the interrelations managing credit, and loans to all of you. It was important for me to understand the workings of our economy as well as those of the legal system for the protection of fundamental rights and those of the protection of consumer rights.

As I said at the beginning of the book, the content presented in this work, is the result of many readings, interviews and research. It also comes from my life experience, a personal journey, but also my work as an advisor. The interventions and helpful support I gave to my clients struggling with so many problems related to the credit system served as documentation and experimental basis. From this process of questioning, reflection and case studies, I came to several hypotheses and conclusions that you have now been exposed to. I did this in respect to my personal style, seeking authenticity, truth and I hope I have managed to capture your interest, making you aware of individual and collective challenges in this area.

Initially I shared my vision and approach to the practices and personal attitudes, in regards to credit. Including the Karpman

Triangle, the intervention model exerted from transactional analysis, a wonderful tool and a valuable and effective aid to help improve one's personal and financial behaviour. The first chapters discussed the functioning of the banking and economic environment during different historical periods. The following chapters focused more specifically on credit by dissecting the ramifications and intricacies of this system. I invite you to sift through the various chapters and choose the information that meets your specific needs. I hope you find potential solutions and answers to your questions and concerns. The aim is also to stimulate readers to awaken and develop awareness on the topics presented and perhaps, in the longer term, stimulate public debate.

THE HIDDEN FACE OF CREDIT : Knowledge is power

Are you forever a slave to money or do you want to become the master of it in order to ensure a better future? Then you must learn to apply the Babylonian Theory or any other action plan for your prosperity. Like many personalities, Jim Rohn[25] experienced bankruptcy, failures and popular disapproval. Then one day, he stopped in order to best consider what he needed to do to change his life. "What's happening to you does not really have an effect on how your life turns out. It's more about what you make of it that decides the outcome in the end" he says in his book "Strategies for Prosperity". He learned from his experience and by avoiding to make the same mistakes he was able to find the right path. He's now become a source of inspiration.

I share with you here some of these choices :

1. Make a plan for prosperity that grows year by year over a period of 10 years;

2. Move away from destructive people who lead you outside your personal targets;

3. Surround yourself with "positive" people, advisors that will help you stay on course, in accordance with your own values;

---

25 Rohn, Jim, 7 Strategies for prosperity, French version, 208 pages

4. Create your present with discipline and know how to say "no" to impulsive offers;

5. Share your commitments with groups who defend just causes;

6. Appreciate happiness without regard to the value of objects, but rather by measuring the wealth of respectful human relations;

7. Experience the feeling of pride when you get out of the worst circumstances while standing on your own;

8. Reaching out to others will ensure that there will always be someone around you, a trustworthy person to reach out to, if one day you need them;

9. Maintain confidence in yourself by acting on three values: discipline, responsibility, action;

10. Take the steps that will make you free to own property without sacrificing your values.

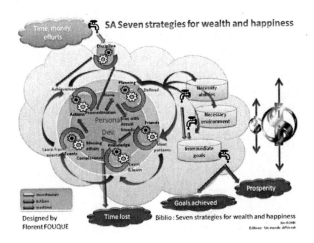

The key to success is a realistic approach to your behaviour and careful planning of your progress. I am not a guru of positive thinking, but I agree with the idea of having a serious action plan and follow it with patience and determination. I give you here my method of clarifying my actions, so that each of my decisions coincides with my goals.

You want more money? Then learn to manage it, to save it and make it grow. Don't wait until you have more money to start managing it differently. The money is managed from the first dollar! The time you take to plan your budget, your purchases, and your decisions is important. Read up on all subjects that will help you become a more informed consumer and negotiate cash purchases on your own behalf instead of relying on credit agencies.

My dearest wish is to help people of good faith put the Babylonian Theory into action and use their money and their savings as a lever for prosperity.

Here is a reminder for you of the simple rules that make up this planning.

Its source: at the time of Babylon, in accordance with the code of laws, every citizen had to prepare their own budget based on their income using a very simple calculation. This calculation will be adapted to our present time and whatever your tax rate, this method applies to all budgets. If you start from a young age to practice this theory, you will be rich in 60 years, even if you work for minimum wage. You will never know personal financial disaster if you rigorously apply this method.

Here is the method of financial wisdom: You must allocate 10 % of your gross income to any form of savings, then 30 % of your gross income should be spent on your credit debt, that is: mortgage payment or rent, car payment , payment of credit card, payment on a personal loan, student loan payment, credit payment, installment payment agreement with a collection agency or any rotary, and finally 60 % of your gross income must be attributed to services, that is to say: income tax, various taxes, home insurance, car insurance, electricity, groceries, car maintenance, home, personal expenses, personal care, transportation costs, school fees and other service charges ...

Postponing your recovery will only complicate things.

Without discipline, it's a growing debt. You may ignore the philosophy of Jim Rohn on the subject: "The poor are people who spend their money and put aside what they have left. The rich are people who put money aside and spend what is left. This is the very same money, only the philosophy is different."

CONCLUSION

A NEW START ON THE ROAD TO PROSPERITY

The topics covered in this book are related to credit and the banking system, they paint a portrait of a complex reality and shed light onto various issues affecting consumers. This state of affairs requires special attention, even significant changes on the part of our leaders and representatives.

Issues related to indebtedness of individuals and an unbalanced and dysfunctional credit system, are situations that require support from our elected officials, our government and all relevant bodies. These decisions are in the public interest because they affect the common good. Debt problems are affecting a growing number of consumers and the inability of our system to be able to offer recovery assistance solutions can only harm a healthy social economy and community development.

An improved system is needed if we do not want to deepen the chasm. Just find statistics on the large number of bankruptcies and households in debt and / or living in poverty. Increasingly, organizations that provide services emergency food, clothing and others are overwhelmed by the increasing demand for basic necessities. This reality must be seen as an indication of a worsening economic situation for the middle class and poor. There is a safe bet that the debt system and abusive credit are, in many cases, the cause of these problems or at the very least, aggravating them.

The necessary changes will require the goodwill and support as well as sustained efforts from our society, starting with individuals as consumers. The emergence of the collective consciousness acknowledging the problem first, then mobilizing motivated consumers to take action on the issues of indebtedness and the credit system. This would constitute a solid basis for initiating a reform movement. This could take the form of a "lobby" made up of groups of consumers, among other actions, submit briefs and requests to the targeted communities. These groups would be supported and guided by experts not affiliated with the financial institutions.

Problems raised here: In terms of important issues that have been discussed in this book, without providing an exhaustive list, let's review the following examples:

- The lack of public awareness and of consumers about the functioning and processes of the credit system.
- The difficulty for consumers to obtain information on their personal credit from information and credit agencies.
- The lack of established structure to assist consumers in respect of credit and debt.
- The banking community's rigid attitude in regards to customers struggling with their debt problems.
- The coalition between the credit agencies and financial institutions to keep the consumer in a state of helplessness and vulnerability as a result of credit problems and debt.
- The absence of "apparent" government and political commitment to engage in the protection of consumers rights in certain cases.
- The judicial process and the Law on the protection of personal information to review in the best interests of consumers and not only those of the credit agencies and the financial community.

The next step, in my opinion. My intention is to provide a logical and complementary follow-up to this book in the form of general as well as specific recommendations in regards to the issues at stake. These recommendations will likely be in the form of a manual, guide or other book. This project will be implemented in the course of the next year if all conditions are favourable. The readers of this book can monitor the progress and offer support and feedback to help in its development.

The first essential recommendation is to ask elected officials and concerned bodies to adopt a policy fostering the protection and improvement of the credit system for consumers. Specific and targeted government guidelines should be developed to address issues affecting the field of credit as well as consumer relationships with the banking community and credit agencies.

Amongst the obstacles and critical areas to identify, it is important to intervene, for example, on the withdrawal of consent issues. You may have noticed while reading this chapter, the problems caused by the use of this procedure and the unfavorable rights it represents to consumers. This issue should be taken into account and concrete solutions should be offered to consumers who in many cases find themselves in legal limbo.

The resolution of this problem and many other situations rests on a political will to engage and initiate changes to government policies, policies with regard to consumer protection, and the amendment or revision of laws or regulations relating to the credit system and conservation of all personal information.

Of course, prevention work and education of the population is also needed. It will require the support of all interested parties from various backgrounds to develop understanding and knowledge of credit and the reflex to integrate better consumer habits at a young age. The schooling system must be arraigned on this chapter. ACEF and other support services available in all regions of Quebec becoming active in wanting to help people learn about how to budget and manage their personal finances.

We can continue this long reflection and identify and explore several possible solutions. But I will stop here, and I reiterate my willingness to offer in the near future, a document containing a series of recommendations that will provide different avenues.

It's your turn to assess. To move forward with personal or professional projects , it is important to set your own goals. Ideally, these objectives must be specified from five characteristics.

To do this, coaches generally apply the SMART method:

- Specific
- Measurable
- Achievable
- Realistic
- Time-bound

For an objective to be specific, you can use action verbs. Finally, an objective is targeted when an end date is established, thereby allowing you to assess at this time, find out what can be improved and redefine a new goal to progress step by step. SMART enables progress and allows us to stay in control of our lives, instead of being at the mercy of the credit agencies.

Must your approach toward credit change after reading this book? Well here are some useful little tips ... or inspiring at the least.

- **Free yourself from debt and reclaim your own management power.**

- **Extend the sphere of your knowledge to become a more informed consumer.**

- **Learn about yourself and discover the pleasure of a change in attitude by focusing on discipline.**

- **Take care of your finances actively, with an ideal budget that will make you reach financial independence.**

- **Weigh your purchases and try to put them to the test of time, instead of succumbing to flashy advertisements.**

- **Surround yourself with people who respect your lifestyle choices and values.**

- **Learn the art of living well by sharing with society what created your wealth, your personality, your generosity, your openness to just causes.**

In closing, I hope with all my heart that you enjoyed this book and that the proposed tools will meet your needs. I would greatly appreciate receiving your testimony at: info@credit-montreal.ca

EPILOGUE
THE SEARCH FOR BALANCE

N ow that you are aware of the rules to the game of Monopoly and you have realized that you are not the pawn on the game board, but the hand holding the pawn, I would venture to add a philosophical note to close this piece. Let's start with a little humor …

THE VIRUS CALLED "IT'S BECAUSE".

It's because of this....it's because of that…

My personal definition of the "it's because" syndrome: mutually transmitted emotional affliction or illness that has the effect of making a human believe that he or she is not responsible for anything and that everything that happens to them is caused by everyone else. Here are the symptoms: psychodrama, financial difficulties, divorce, bankruptcy and a state of emotional distress.

You probably hear a lot of people say, "what happened to me today is because of him or because of her." In the long term, this type of behavior leads human beings to fail and, unfortunately in many cases to states of severe depression.

If a particular situation in your present life, brings you to emotional distress or failure, it's probably because, at one point in the past you made a decision based on an emotion that tied into a psychodramatic emotional triangle or on a false belief. You acted on the sudden emotion, without discernment and without putting your judgment in action.

Doubt, fear and confusion caused you to violate your scale of values and make an irrational decision based on your emotions. Therefore, you find yourself in a state of emotional suffering that will affect your financial situation.

Experience and time have allowed me to understand that the cycle of life tends towards continuous evolution. In my view, life is based on repetitive cycles leading to the improvement of the species in order for it to survive. Therefore, in principle, if you base your lifestyle on the rhythm of constantly evolving to become a better person, your whole life will be a success on all levels.

If you take the path of involution rather than evolution, your life will become a series of difficult times that will make you aware of the need to resume the path of evolution. In the medical field, it is said that a cell that closes on itself dies (involution cycle). When you row a boat against the current of a river, you need to double your physical efforts to advance until you understand which direction the current is going, then you can allow yourself to a go with the flow. As Gilles Vigneault said: *"It's by going Up the river, that we learn in which direction the water flows "*.

As evolution is a principle of nature, involution, in turn, leads us to live a state of suffering that will force us back to evolution. As soon as we leave the path of balance, life takes care to send us back in the right way that is evolution.

We must stop blaming others for our misfortunes and become aware of our responsibilities towards our decisions.

Some people seek happiness throughout their lives through glory, power and equity. But once they arrive at the top they realize that they are just as unhappy as before with indeed some small emotional compensation , and that all they have achieved, glorified or owned was in fact an illusion. This is the difference between **success** in life and a **successful** life.

I've known people who believed that having a house would make them happy. Once in the house, they believed that having a child, then two and three would make them happy. Then a bigger house, a swimming pool, cottage and so on, and finally they reached a divorce or bankruptcy. They believed that happiness was in the future when in fact, it is in the present moment, here and now.

MY RECIPE FOR HAPPINESS AND FINANCIAL SUCCESS

Here are some thoughts related to each ingredient of my "happiness" recipe which I hope will provide you with important keys to achieving yours.

1. Living in the moment

Are you able to walk on the sidewalk constantly looking behind you (= in the past)? Of course not, you wouldn't see the obstacles in front of you and you would risk tripping over something and hurting yourself. What would therefore be the lesson of this experience for you? Look ahead while walking! Otherwise you're going to hurt yourself (= suffering). Leave the past behind you, move forward now. Make a clean break with the past, and move forward...

Are you able to walk on the sidewalk and look at to the sky while doing so? Of course not!! You can't see where you put your feet and you may stumble and hurt yourself. So the moral of this story is to look ahead of you in the present to see what happens. If you pay attention to your eye physiology, you will notice that your eyes cover a peripheral field of vision of 180 degrees left-right and up-down 130 degrees. In my opinion, nature has provided us so that we can see what is present before us and not what is behind us.

For living life in the present moment, I recommend Eckart Tolle's book: The Power of Now.

Become aware of your surroundings. Happiness is not something to be achieved in the future, but a perpetual state which lives in the now.. It is important to understand that there are only four things you control in your life. You have no control over the rest.

You control:

- Your gestures ,
- your words,
- your thoughts,
- your actions.

So, to live in the present moment, we must take action on what we can control here and now... and apply this rule all the time. Achieving this state of balance allows you to coordinate healthy living and spiritual growth without forgetting financial stability.

2. Achieving financial balance

To achieve the much sought after financial balance, put into practice the Babylonian Theory. This budgetary practice ensures that you will have the money ahead of you and you will never have to tolerate a job you don't like or a hateful boss. So you do not have to deny your values and who you are, for money. Depression begins the day you give up your values and you cease to respect yourself . In my opinion, depression is a starting point to return to equilibrium.

Many people live in the world of appearance, they think they can find happiness in the possession of assets, yet one should not envy them, because one day, just like you, they will realize that happiness is not necessarily found there.

Humans learn by experience. Knowledge is the understanding and awareness of the experience. We shouldn't believe the old religious adage that says to go to heaven one must be poor.

This is completely false. You can live in prosperity and experience happiness. You can be a spiritual person and be rich materially. Conversely, you can live modestly and experience happiness. The difference is that happiness lies in a state of being connected to the fullness and joy and only in the present moment. The majority of people believe that it is social recognition that brings happiness.

In fact, they confuse it with pleasure.

Pleasure is an important motivation, *but short-lived* for a human being, it can also prove to be an emotional compensation, a trap in the guise of satisfying one's real needs and therefore an obstacle to deep happiness. Happiness is permanent and pleasure is temporary.

For example, I noticed that many people carry out this false belief through their way of consuming: one must have, in order to be. The underlying message conveyed by this popular belief is that that "you have to work to get what you have." Once this asset is acquired you will be admired, this illusory person you want to be in the future and you wish to project to others. In fact, this belief tends to feed your desire for social recognition and nothing more.

Today, with my experience, I can say that one must be authentic and that "having" will come to you. The opposite will probably lead to repeated failures and you will experience difficulties both emotional and financial until you have regained balance. If you think "one must have" in order to "be", I'd say, you might live in illusion.

3. SPIRITUAL GROWTH

Over the past centuries and the fact that many people were illiterate , religions have contributed to civilizing human beings. But what about the deep meaning of the word religion which comes from the Latin word religare, which means "to connect with God"? For all those who practice a religion (whether Muslim, Christian or Buddhist ...), there could certainly be common ground in saying that "all believe" in a supreme creator of the universe.

In my view, if your religion preaches the values of the heart, you will be lead to experience love, goodness and service to others. If your religion teaches a doctrine that advocates the values of the mind, you will want to divide and conquer, rule over others, you will be tempted to impose your dogma onto others and act in the name of God.

The mental state of imbalance used in religious environments sometimes brings a man into experiencing the psychodrama of the persecutor/saviour/victim. This promotes hatred and causes the "it's because" syndrome that pushes individuals to act on behalf of God, acts of madness or terrorism. Where of the extremist or fundamentalist.

Believing, is often the hope that a theory or dogma is true without having experienced it. Thus the wise ones say that we should not believe in something without first experiencing it. I invite you to believe only in what you have experienced. You will certainly be closer to your own truth.

The values that advocate the way of the heart are in my humble opinion, those that elevate you to the best of what you are or in becoming unconditional love. To achieve spiritual balance, we must devote time to prayer or meditation, allowing quality time for yourself, creating space for the "higher self", in the heart of one's life. Furthermore, in my view , spirituality comes through humility, nobility, gratitude, selflessness and also through the art of knowing how to listen. Spirituality is the highest level of consciousness in humans. It is personal to each one of us and must remain so.

My own code of honor, is therefore based on these values:

- Always tell the truth, even if it costs me my life,
- protect the weakest and most vulnerable,
- love and serve my neighbor,
- devote my life to a just and altruistic cause,
- work for peace in the world.

To have peace in the heart, is to experience the values of the heart and let Providence cloak you with its beatitudes.

- **Being of service for a just cause**

This is to devote your efforts and time to serve a cause dear to your heart, it can be volunteering at a center for people with disabilities, spend time with people who have no family, etc...

In my case, it is to assist consumers in their economic difficulties so that they can regain their financial and emotional balance to free themselves from the shackles of debt. This relational approach often allows the consumer to take charge and become a more informed consumer.

I believe that our government should provide tax credits for volunteers for the hours worked. Thus, more people would devote themselves to a cause and communities would do much better. Encouraging and promoting such actions could be very constructive. We have a large number of baby boomers who will be retiring shortly. Society could greatly benefit from their wisdom and experience. Moreover, as an example, the Ministry of Education of Ontario provides credit to students who give their time to charity or do volunteer work. What a great initiative!

I have a story about this. One day an Aboriginal Elder asked me the following question:

– *"Would you perceive the illusion of the white man for a moment?*
– *Of course, I said.*

He continued:

– Do the four elements (water, fire, air and earth) that constitute nature acknowledge borders between countries, provinces and cities?
– *Of course not! I said.*

He asked again:

– Do animals also acknowledge these borders?
– *Uh, no ...*

– Do the trees, plants and minerals acknowledge these borders ...?
– *Uh ... no I said.*

Then he looked at me and said:

– Now, are all the elements, plants, animals and minerals subject to the law of white men?"

After a moment of reflection, I thought that if the government wrote a law to tax the trees or rocks, the latter would not even flinch one bit because human law has no effect on them. Even if I taxed or fined a tree for being on the border of my land, it wouldn't move, I would have to cut it down to assert my position.

The wise man replied:

"Brave young man, the law of the white man has no effect on nature or anything because it exists only in his imagination and in his head! And he firmly believes that this illusion really exists. The white men have created laws to organize themselves in society and deprive their neighbors in order to control their fellow humans, because they lack maturity and wisdom in their hearts and in their minds."

The wise elder added, "When nature is unleashed, borders do not exist and the law of men either; natural balance returns to its rightful place!"

"The illusion created by the mind that veils your eyes is the symbol of darkness that hides the truth."

I found these to be very wise words and I wanted to share them with you as I conclude this work. May this book be a means to shed light on the hidden face of a reality that has perhaps imprisoned you on your path. If so, I now give you the key to your freedom.

ACKNOWLEDGEMENTS

The creation of this book would not have been possible without the love and support of my loving wife Danica who has supported me throughout my research over the past decade. My involvement in multiple movements, hundreds of conferences and numerous readings often kept me away from my family. If this book is a bestseller, the profits will be used to compensate for the missed time with my family for the time allocated to this cause ... Thank you, my dear, for supporting me even in the most difficult moments when I sometimes wanted to give up...

A special thanks to my friend Denis Tessier for his moral and spiritual support in the implementation of this book . Many thanks to Claire Crépeau who lodged me during the writing of these lines, thank you to Margaret M. for her teachings and coaching. Thank you Maryse Pichette for lending me your desk and chair for writing, because without knowing it, you greatly inspired me. Thank you to Yves D'Avignon, Anjulie Saliba and Nicole Guindon for the final editing. Special thanks to Yvonne Senechal, Marjorie Theodore and Dr. Mohamed Benkhalifa for their support and presence. Thank you to all those who have directly or indirectly contributed to this book.

Thank you to my uncle Lucien, whom I love so much, thank you to my mother for her support, thank you to all the great men who inspired me ... Pierre Therrien, Jacques Lavigueur, thank you to Louciano Esposto and Gabriel Génarelli , thank you to Michael Salotti , thank you Serge Jarry, thank you to Claude Paquette, Fabrice Barré, Josée Bonneau, Eric Bisson, Stéphane Toupin and many others ...

Thank you to all those people who supported me when I fell, thank you to my life teachers whom, by treachery, deceit, hatred, envy, jealousy and suffering, have made me grow in experience and wisdom.

MORE ABOUT THE AUTHOR AND HIS INTENTIONS

Dear reader,

I am one of those who aspire to a better world and all that is beautiful, good and true. Born in Montreal in April 1970, I grew up in Saint-Hubert and Longueuil, Quebec. I did my secondary education at the André-Laurendeau school where I completed my secondary IV and, in all humility, I am one of those dropouts who did not complete high school. I thus consider myself as an autodidact. I was a seeker of truth all my life, but towards the age of 30 I started to get interested in everything related to the foundation of law. I am among those who believe that to find the truth, one must go to the origin of things. I once wished I was a lawyer and would surely have been an excellent litigator, but disputing cases did not appeal to me, the basis of the origin of law however, very much does. I am passionnate about discovering the "why" and the "how".

I worked for several years in the automotive field from sales to financing as well as second chance financing. I experienced years of glory as well as years of difficulty and challenges that were, in retrospect, very rewarding experimentation.

During the years in this environment I met great men who inspired me by their charisma and their righteousness. I also experienced some of the worst villains, all of which were, also, my life teachers ...

I went from the bottom of the ladder through what is called the University of the streets. My family also went through these crises, but my parents taught me good moral values. I charged through life with limited tools and resources. But in reality, today, I can tell you how it was enriching to learn from my trials and errors. Currently, in my work, I help people struggling with financial problems. It has become a passion for me, but also a noble cause of helping to raise the fallen.

I, too, went through the financial desert and I went bankrupt. That's why I understand what some of you are experiencing.

Each person that I receive in my office is heard without judgment and with great compassion. I work for humans and not to feed and fatten the system.

If what I do, can become a source of inspiration for others, when I leave this world, I will leave with the feeling of having done something for humanity, to make it a little bit better.

> *"The greatest quality of a revolutionary is love*
> **Ernesto Che Guevara**

I believe we, as a society, are at a crossroads. In my opinion, either humanity rises to collective consciousness, or our civilization is doomed to destruction within a few decades. Excessive capitalism, consumerism, personal glory, the quest for power and the notion of possession are old defense mechanisms and must now give way to the security provided by the support of the community along with better values, such as altruism.

These values have no place in a society evolving in consciousness. We notice every day that truths are revealed in broad daylight, people are tired of small shenanigans of those who govern us and those companies that fill their pockets at the expense of the environment. I think it will continue to grow. The first transformation must initially come from within each and everyone of us, and then spread to the community and then the political level. John F. Kennedy said: *"Ask not what your country can do for you but what you can do for your country!"*

Righteousness, love, justice, and service are the foundation on which our founding fathers aspired to build the system of democracy so that their children and future generations, could benefit from allowing access to future happiness, liberty, fraternity and equality. The values we now recognize in our society are those that come from illusion, namely: image, envy, betrayal, jealousy, selfishness, lying, looking for recognition, power, control, racism, division, abuse, violence and so on ...

Today, I finished writing this book to share with you the

experience and knowledge I have acquired over the past fifteen years and has opened my eyes. I am a seeker of truth who longs for a better world. Of course, in our lives, we must sometimes touch the bottom of the ocean in order to be able to rise to the surface. And this, is what we are collectively experiencing at this moment in time.

That is why I joined the United Nations 7 Billion Actions campaign to be an agent and advocate for solutions and change for the emergence of a better world. Inspired by the United Nations campaign I set myself a goal to take one action per day to change the world. This book is a contribution in that direction.

I am involved with various organizations and I act as chairman at the UNAK or United Nations of Aboriginals of Kanada. The main mission of this organization is to support young unmarried mothers and single mothers to return to today's society while maintaining their ancestral traditional values. In short, I invite you to visit the Web site at www.unak2012.ca

BIBLIOGRAPHY

YUNUS, Muhammad; *Creating a World without Poverty,*
Banker for the poor, Nobel Peace prize in 2006,
Éditions Le livre de poche

HILL, Napoleon; *Think and grow rich,*
Éditions de l'Homme

DI MARTINO, Michel; *Guide pratique financier pour
l'entrepreneur,*
Éditions Eyrolles

MORIN, Edgar; *La voie, pour l'avenir de l'humanité,*
Éditions Fayard

COHEN, Daniel; *Wealth of the World and Poverty
of Nations,*
Éditions Flammarion

MICHAUD, Yves; *Les raisons de la colère,*
Éditions Fides

NADEAU, Alain-Robert: *Vie privée et droits fondamentaux,*
Éditions Carswell

ACEF; *Guide Couple et argent, où en sommes-nous,*
www.cosommateurs.qc.ca/acef

CLASON, George S; *The Richest Man in Babylon,*
Éditions Un monde différent

ROHN, Jim; *strategies for Wealth & Happiness,*
Éditions Un monde différent

ROBBINS, Anthony; *Awaken the Giant Within,*
Un monde différent

LAUZON, Léo-Paul, *Contes et comptes du prof Lauzon,*
Éditions Michel Brûlé

AIDE-MEMOIRE

My personal notes: _____
_____
_____
_____
_____
_____
_____
_____
_____
_____
_____
_____

My personal goals: _____
_____
_____
_____
_____
_____
_____
_____
_____
_____
_____
_____
_____

To contact

SYLVAIN PAQUETTE

www.bucc.ca

This book is also available in digital format.

www.enlibrairie-aqei.com

AQÉI

Finished printing in Canada
In August 2014